OUT OF THE CROWD

David W. Jones

For Etta and Bob
Carrie, Cayla, Abbie, and Nathan.

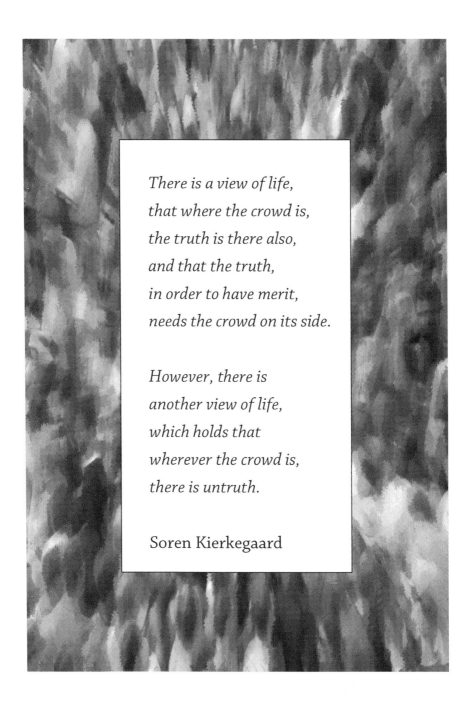

There is a view of life,
that where the crowd is,
the truth is there also,
and that the truth,
in order to have merit,
needs the crowd on its side.

However, there is
another view of life,
which holds that
wherever the crowd is,
there is untruth.

Soren Kierkegaard

Contents

Introduction

This is a crowd.

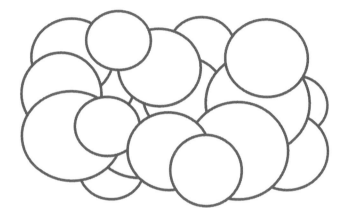

Look at it again.

Which circle in the crowd is you?

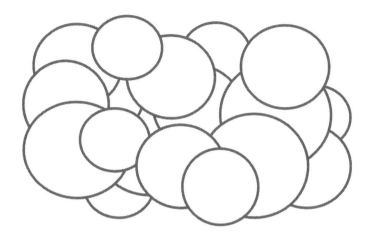

Can't find yourself?

Of course not. It's just a bunch of circles. None of them look like you. Even if you had a circle that was you, or represented you, because they are bunched together and look alike, you'd have a hard time picking your circle from the rest. That's the nature of a crowd. As an individual in a crowd, you blend in, you become indistinguishable from the group.

This book is about coming out of the crowd.

Coming out of the crowd looks something like this.

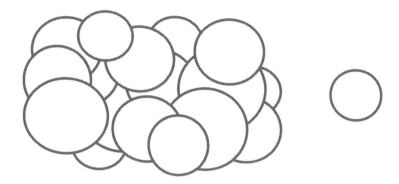

Seems simple enough.

Actually, it is quite hard. Crowds are everywhere and can potentially permeate all our groups. A crowd can be as large as a nation of millions or as small as you and one or two others. Your school can be a crowd; the people you work with can be a crowd; your neighborhood can be a crowd; your family can be a crowd; the family you left decades ago can be a crowd. Any group you're connected to can be a crowd. You may even have a crowd inside your head. The crowd is any group where the emotional lines of connection overlap like the image above.

Deciding to live differentiated from your crowds, to be a single one in relation to the numerous, to have an "I" in the midst of the many, will be both a challenge and a choice you have to make over and again to come out of the crowd.

Separating from your crowds will take more than changing your address, your membership, or your mindset, and if you can differentiate yourself from your crowds, they may or may not let you go without a struggle. Maybe they will. Maybe they will just send you on your merry way and not think of you again, filling your vacancy with someone else or just merging the group to cover whatever holes you leave. However, they may do more than notice, more than comment, more than express their displeasure; they may come after you. They may come after you physically or simply emotionally as they resist any effort you make to set yourself apart from the group. Though it likely will be very intense, it is actually not personal. It is just what crowds do.

Even though it is risky and may introduce you to pain in a way you have not felt before, and even though it may seem at the beginning like you are in an isolated desert of loneliness, it will all be worth it. For yourself, for those you care about, and for all the others who've lost themselves in the crowd, all the effort will be worthwhile.

A Simple Crowd

You and I are different. The people in your life are different from the people in my life. As I am different from you, so is each person in your life different from you, too. That's why they are called 'others.' It may seem odd to point that out, but crowds encourage the denial of our otherness. In a crowd we can forget just how particular each of us is.

Even though you and I are different from all others, crowds, however, are not so different. Philosophers, theologians, psychologists, and sociologists have talked about crowds for thousands of years. They have used different terms like: *collective, system, herd, mass, mob, enmeshed system, fused emotional group,* and *the world.* I'm going to use *crowd* as did the writers of The Gospels of Matthew, Mark, Luke and John, as well as philosophers like Tactitus, Epicurus, and Kierkegaard, along with Sociologist Gustave LeBon, and Poet Ralph Waldo Emerson. Each of them had their crowds, as you have yours and I have mine. Though we live in different parts of the earth and different eras, the crowds that affected them had some of the same characteristics as our crowds, as all crowds, herds, mobs, and collectives do.

For an orientation, here is a simple, easily observable, well-known crowd. Can you recognize it by this image?

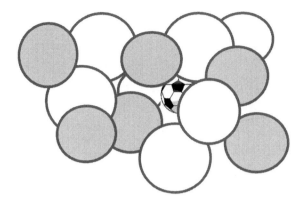

Know what it is?

I'll give you a hint, they gather regularly in streets, yards, and fields across the world. They can organize themselves or be in a community structured league. This crowd is a frenzied pair of five year old children's soccer teams (to use the U.S. term for the game).

Perhaps you are familiar with beginners playing soccer and their tendency to swarm around the ball, chasing it around the field, merging into an active, passionate, emotional herd. If not, I hope you can imagine it for those herds show many of the characteristics that crowds exhibit.

Here is another image. These two groups aren't crowds at all. These are older, more experienced, more mature players who have a better understanding of the game, how it is played, and their personal roles on their teams.

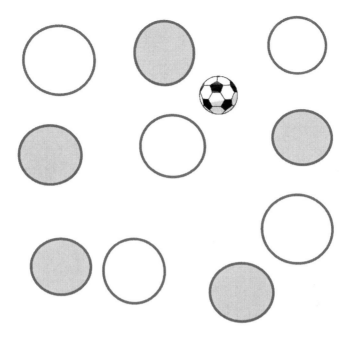

If you look at the two diagrams, you can see the difference between the five year olds in their herd and the mature players in their teams.

The most obvious difference between the two is spacing. The more mature players understand that space between them is important. Space between players in soccer is as important as space between musical notes in a song. If there is no space between notes in music, there is no distinguishable rhythm, tempo, or song, only a long blurry noise. In the younger, less mature groups, there is a lot of rampant activity, a lot of bumping, and kicking, but little soccer actually happens because they have not yet learned the importance of roles and spacing required in order to function as a team.

So, too, is it in your life. If you are going to live out your particular calling, your particular self, your particular identity, you need emotional, intellectual, and social space between your self and others. Without healthy spacing and clear boundaries distinguishing you from others, your music, your song, your life, your role will be smothered, absorbed, blended into the greater group, the crowd.

Here is a helpful question you may have seen long ago.

Why fit in when you were born to stand out?

That question came from the wise soul of Dr. Seuss who also offered this advice,

Today you are You,
that is truer than true.
There is no one alive who is
Youer than You.

Your friends, family, groups, clubs, congregations, nations, if they are healthy, will give you the space, the nurture, the encouragement to differentiate yourself, to grow, learn, mature, risk, reach, question, try. If they don't, if they encourage you to fit in at the expense of your soul, or lose the you that is you for the sake of the group, then they are just crowds.

Before we go on, think about your groups and consider the previous two images of the soccer teams I showed you. Do your relationships feel more like the reactive image of the young five-year-old players or the more mature response-able older players?

Jesus and Crowds

Jesus didn't like crowds.

In the Gospel of Mark, the oldest of the New Testament gospels, Jesus was constantly on the move. Mark often wrote, "Immediately..." Jesus taught, healed, prayed, and then "immediately" left for some other destination. Why was he moving so often? The crowds.

If you map Jesus' travels, his journeying seems erratic, sometimes wandering from one place to another and back. Why did Jesus seldom choose direct routes? The crowds.

When Jesus healed someone, he consistently instructed, "Don't tell anyone." Or if proclaimed, "The Messiah," he instructed the spirits or people to keep quiet. Why keep his identity a secret? The crowds.

As Jesus travelled throughout Israel and the surrounding territories, the crowd seemed to have been chasing him, forming and reforming from the beginning, Mark 1,

> That evening, around sunset, when it was getting dark, people were bringing so many to him who were sick that the whole city was crowded outside the door.
>
> In the morning, before sunrise, Jesus got up and went to an isolated place to be by himself and pray. When the crowd formed, looking for Jesus, Simon and the other disciples got nervous, so they went and found Jesus where he was praying.
>
> "Everyone is searching for you," Simon told him.
>
> "Let's go somewhere else, so that I may proclaim the gospel there, also. That is why I came." And they left.

Jesus took time away from everyone, to be with God. While he was away, the crowd looked for him. Simon (later called Peter) and the other new disciples of Jesus got nervous. The crowd wanted to know where Jesus was, and they expected these new followers to produce him. The rookie disciples reacted to the desire and demand of the crowd while Jesus did not. Instead, Jesus moved on away from them.

Here is a brief summary of the progressing conflict Jesus had with the crowds in the book of Mark. In Mark 2, the crowd was so large it kept some from bringing their paralyzed friend to Jesus. In Mark 4, the crowd was so large that Jesus had to get into a boat to give himself enough space to be seen and heard by the people on the shore. In Mark 5, the crowd "pressed" in on Jesus so much he had a hard time moving. In Mark 7, Jesus pulled people out of the crowds before healing them. In Mark 10, the crowd tried to prevent a blind man from being healed. In Mark 11, the crowd shouted praises as Jesus came into Jerusalem, but their adoration for him turned nasty by Mark 14 as the crowd came with Judas to arrest Jesus. In Mark 15, the intensity increased as Jesus was held before Pilate and the crowd shouted, "Crucify him!" Pilate was pressured by the crowd and turned Jesus over to be killed. The crowd jeered at Jesus as he died on the cross.

Sociologist Gustave LeBon described the power of the crowd over individuals, "An individual in a crowd is a grain of sand, which the wind stirs up at will." Throughout the gospels, crowds blow through towns and cities like Nazareth and Jerusalem, through holy spaces like Synagogues and The Temple, through the power structures including political leaders like Herod and Pilate, and through the religious leaders like the Pharisees and the Sadducees. Crowds even transform Jesus' family into a barrier he has to overcome.

Jesus faced every crowd, from the family circle to the malicious mob as the unwavering "I am." In the gospels, no one stands in relationship to people in their often-storming crowds and maintains his or her individuality, integrity, and identity like Jesus. Jesus achieved "The Greatest Human Accomplishment" as described by Ralph Waldo Emerson,

To be yourself in a world that is constantly trying to make you something else is the greatest accomplishment.

Jesus didn't like crowds, and after they got to know him for who he was, they rejected him as the unwavering "I" as Barbara Brown Taylor relates,

> *Jesus died because he would not stop being who he was and who he was was very upsetting. He turned everything upside down. He allied himself with the wrong people and insulted the right ones. He disobeyed the law. He challenged the authorities who warned him to stop. The government officials warned him to stop. The religious leaders warned him to stop. And when he would not stop, they had him killed, because he would not stop being who he was.*
>
> *At any point along the way, he could have avoided the cross... He could have stopped being who he was, but he did not. When the soldiers showed up in the garden to arrest him, he did not disappear into the dark. He stepped into the light of their torches and asked them whom they were looking for. "Jesus of Nazareth," they answered him, and he said, "I am he."*

Only those overly familiar with Jesus can ignore him or make him into an endorser and champion for our crowds dressing him up in the costumes we've adorned for ourselves. To face one who stands out while we take our place in line and chase the latest fad stirs us in unsettling ways when we are comfortable being settled. If we can attend to his presence, to who he is and how he is, we can't help but feel afraid for he is like no other.

Far more frightening than a preacher by the river shouting hellfire and damnation is one who on a cross says, "Father, forgive them, they don't know what they're doing." Far more frightening than a teacher who knows all the answers before you can even ask the questions is a teacher who questions the answers you've centered your world upon. Far more frightening than a politician who seeks your money is one who says your greatest treasure has little lasting value. Far more frightening than a king who comes to take over a city on a warhorse leading soldiers in a parade is one who comes on a donkey preceded by children. Far more frightening than a general who calls for weapons is one who commands they be put away. More frightening than a warrior who cannot be killed is one who can die so easily – then will not stay dead!

We may try to cage him in a creed, an ideology, a worship format, a Sunday time slot, in history long ago, in a stone covered grave, or on a throne high above us in a heavenly realm, but he keeps coming to us repeatedly, daring us to do far more than believe, challenging us to become.

According to an ancient fable, we are like orphaned tiger cubs who have been adopted by goats. We live day to day, along with the herd. We learn the language of the goats, eat what they eat, run when they run, bleat loudly when they are upset. As far as we know, we are goats, yet, somehow we feel we are not near what we were created to become.

One day, a tiger comes out of the forest and the goats scatter, leaving us alone to fend for ourselves. We freeze, too frightened to run, certain we are about to die. We stare at the tiger. He roars. Our bodies shake. We tremble and bleat out for mercy hoping he will just go away.

The tiger speaks, and to our surprise, we understand him. He asks, "Why are you cubs acting like goats?"

Not one of us responds. Why wouldn't we act like goats?

The king tiger opens his mouth, but instead of devouring us, he grabs us by the scuff of our necks and carries us to the river. We look at our reflection and at him. Is he who we are? Is he who we might become?

Building off this image, Frederick Buechner wrote,

(A) Christian is one who has seen the tiger. "In the juvenescence of the year," T. S. Eliot wrote, "comes Christ the Tiger," and it is a wonderful so much rubbish. Not the soulful-eyed, sugar-sweet, brilliantined Christ of the terrible pictures that one can buy. But this explosion of a man, this explosion of Life itself into life.

We look at him. We glance up from our grazing for a moment, and there he stands, and suddenly we see what a tiger looks like, what a human being really looks like, and if we thought that our goathood was a problem before, our own half-baked, cockeyed humanity, we reach the point here, if we look hard, where the contrast becomes so painful that one or the other of us simply has to go. Either we crucify the tiger just to escape his terrible gaze, or we at least risk the crucifixion of our own goathood, which must go if it is to be replaced by tigerhood. In either case, our first cry when we see him is a cry of woe: if this is what it really is to be human, then what am I? If this is true life, then what is this that I am living?

The Better Love

We like crowds. We like the attention of crowds. We use the ability of drawing a crowd as a measure of success. Churches seek big crowds at worship. Singers want big crowds at concerts. Retailers hope for big crowds at their stores. For many, churches included, crowds are money. P.T. Barnum noted, "Every crowd has a silver lining."

Jesus' vision was different, which is why Jesus did not set catering to crowds as his goal. Instead, he saw the mob and the mob mentality as a barrier. He had another way of measuring success, a different way of relating, one that is still foreign to us today. As Barbara Penwarden observed,

> *Should a stable manger cradle*
> *the world's hopes in so fragile a form?*
>
> *Should a maker of worlds become*
> *a carpenter's apprentice?*
>
> *Should a king become*
> *a servant to the least of society?*
>
> *The humility of God Incarnate*
> *was no disguise of a majesty*
> *that was too great for us to bear,*
> *but rather the revelation of a majesty*
> *too unlike us to be recognized.*

So, just what was Jesus' way and what did it look like? It's easier to diagram what Jesus' way wasn't. It didn't look like this:

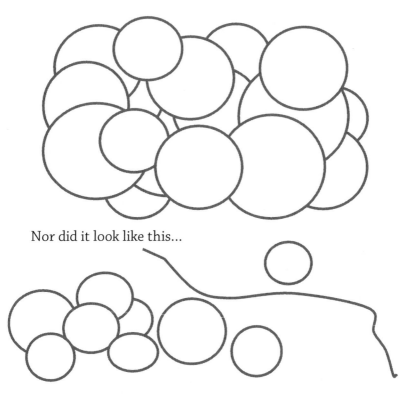

Nor did it look like this...

Look closely at the circle off to the right. Do you know who that is? He lived in Jesus' day, ate bugs and honey, dressed in a camel hair coat, and baptized by the Jordan River. Right, John the Baptist. (The squiggly line is the river.) John separated from the crowd by distancing himself. He lived apart from others out in the desert. People came to him, and John preached at them. John saw people as groups, and labeled them, "Sinners," or worse, "A Brood of Vipers." John lived apart and developed a lifestyle that would keep people away, after all, who wants to live in the desert, wear camels' hair, and eat locusts even if there is honey to go with them? That's not coming out of the crowd. That's just coming away from the crowd. Ralph Waldo Emerson described the difference,

> *It is easy in the world to live after the world's opinions; it is*
> *easy in solitude to live after your own; but the great (person) is*

24

(the one) who in the midst of the crowd keeps with perfect sweetness the independence of solitude.

Jesus did not come out of the crowds by separating like John the Baptist. Jesus didn't have to isolate from people to keep his integrity. Instead he lived as a mind awake in a typically mindless mass. He was in the world but not of the world, in the crowd but not consumed by it. Jesus didn't even let John address him in a group but came to John as a person. While John branded groups, Jesus spoke to particular persons which leads us to the central characteristic of Jesus' way in the world. While John labeled, Jesus loved, but with a different type of love than John or the crowds understood.

Two Forms of Love

In the crowd and in Jesus we see two distinctly different forms of love. Both can be wonderful, joyful, and exciting. Both can also be puzzling, overwhelming, and painful. Both can give life meaning and can make any particular day a memorable day. However, one form of love will pull you into crowd after crowd, losing your soul hoping for validation and approval. The other, the one we see in Jesus, can set you free from your crowds and help you liberate others.

Value Recognizing Love

Value recognizing love is a beautiful type of love. When we 'fall in love,' we are experiencing value recognizing love. We love what we see in another. This love marks, observes, notes, appreciates, and celebrates value. As the saying goes, "Beauty is in the eyes of the beholder." This love appreciates what it beholds as worthwhile and valuable. To someone you love, you may say, "You are so beautiful." "You are so strong." "You are so smart." In doing so, we show our appreciation for the person's beauty, strength, and intelligence. We say words that all of us want to hear, "I find value in you!" "I love you because of who you are." "I love being with you." When it is mutual, the other person becomes a mirror for you to see yourself in a positive light. "I love you," means, "I love the value I see in you"

Sports fans show value recognizing love. When a football team wins, people show up at the airport to welcome them home. "You are so amazing!" "You're the greatest!" "We love you!" "Yeah!" Winning feels great for players and fans alike. However, when the football team loses, and loses repeatedly, the fans don't come. They don't see value. No one shows up at the airport and says, "You are so average!" "You are actually less than par!" "We love you!" When a team loses, there is no love because there is no achievement therefore no value to be recognized. In value recognizing love, perceived value leads to appreciation while lack of value produces no appreciation. No value = no feelings or bad feelings.

Lives lived in search of value recognizing love alone are tragic. Elizabeth KublerRoss summed up life lived under value recognizing love,

> *Most of us have been raised as prostitutes. I will love you "if." And this word "if" has ruined or destroyed more lives than anything else on this planet earth. It prostitutes us; it makes us feel that we can buy love with good behavior, or good grades.*

Regardless of our crowd, in a value recognizing approach to love we hope that through enough fame, fortune, achievement, success, or just all around being 'good', some group will affirm, appreciate, and love us as valuable. But no crowd will. Crowds are incapable. Crowds do not see individuals apart from the roles they play in the group. They see only images, pseudo representations of persons. They cannot value what they cannot perceive. As a result, value-recognizing love will always be ultimately disappointing. Fortunately, there is another type of love, a love the crowd does not comprehend.

Value Giving Love

William Sloan Coffin attributed God's love as a value giving love,

> *Of God's love we can say two things: it is poured out universally for everyone from the Pope to the loneliest wino on the planet; and secondly, God's love doesn't seek value, it creates value. It is not because we have value that we are loved, but because we are loved that we have value. Our value is a gift, not an achievement.*

Value giving love doesn't recognize value, it gives value. It doesn't require; it offers. It doesn't demand; it empowers. Value giving love is the type of love Jesus saw from God and tried to show and teach to others.

In 1615, Galileo Galilei offered the church a gift which the church refused to open. Galileo used a telescope to explore the theory of Copernicus that the earth wasn't the center of the universe but instead rotated around the sun. The church told him to hush and stop promoting such blasphemous ideas. They told all others to abandon his teachings. The religious leaders feared, if the earth wasn't the center of the universe, then how could God love people?

Their question was asked by the author of Psalm 8 two thousand years earlier in a prayer,

> *Gazing at the skies, the works of your hands,*
> *the moon and the stars with all you've created*
> *I wonder, "Who are we that you are mindful of us?*
> *Mortals that You care for us at all?"*

Perhaps a little more attention to Galileo could have helped the church lighten up and not take itself so seriously and then the rest of us might do the same. It certainly may have helped John the Baptist and other value recognizing lovers. Before John encountered Jesus, he preached about his coming this way in Matthew 3,

> *"There is someone coming after me who is far superior to me. I am not even worthy to serve as his servant carrying his sandals. While I baptize you with water for repentance, he will baptize you with fire and the Holy Spirit. He will judge us all as worthy or unworthy, separating us as at harvest, taking the wheat into the granary, but the chaff he will throw into the fire!"*

Then when Jesus' arrived at the River Jordan and wanted John to baptize him, John refused.

> *I'm not worthy to baptize you. You should baptize me.*

JESUS!

Everyone Else

John thought of people in terms of a rising scale based on worthiness. At the top was Jesus, and then downward to include everyone else at the bottom. In John's hierarchy, because of who Jesus' was, John didn't see himself as worthy to carry his dirty, desert dusty sandals.

Value recognizing love requires some sort of recognizable worth to be love worthy. In the mindset of this love, some peopled universe must revolve around him or her as proof of significance.

For Jesus, it wasn't a question of whether or not he was worthier than John or some were worthier than others, personal worth or value were irrelevant in the love that he was bringing. Value recognizing love centers on the loved. Value giving love centers on the lover. If God is mindful of humanity at all, it has little to do with who we are, and much more to do with who and how God is.

Jesus was able to be so wonderfully human because he had nothing to prove. He didn't need John's reference on his resume'. He didn't need certification from The Temple or citizen ship from Rome. God was his resume, certifier, and validator, from the beginning. He was beloved, so he could go into the world loved, loveable, and loving, free from having to justify his value. After his baptism, Jesus went into the desert where the devil challenged him, "If you are God's child," or, "If you are beloved, then prove it." Jesus refused. Apparently, he had better things to do than try to convince the devil or anyone else of anything.

Jesus taught in Matthew 7,

Don't judge or you'll just judge yourself.

When we rate others on worthiness, we only show the scale that we ourselves live under. When we judge others on their value, we show that we only understand a love that recognizes value. For Jesus, worthiness was irrelevant. If God only loves based on a scale of belief, righteousness, or purity, then how is God different from the rest of us? If God is just a supreme rater of value, who cannot love without first recognizing some distinguishing specialness in a group of people based on birth, belief, or ability, then how is God different? If God loves with a value recognizing love, then not only is the life and teaching of Jesus not Good News, it is not even news at all for it is far from new.

Fortunately, Jesus was not only Galilean, he was Galileoan. Neither you nor I have to be the center of any universe for God to love us. God loves like the sun shines as described in this poem by Hafiz,

Even after all this time
the sun never says to the earth,
"You owe me."

Look what happens
with a love like that.
It lights the whole sky.

Not everybody believes in God, in love, or even the sun, I suppose. I don't want to convince you otherwise, but Jesus pointed to the warmth of a different center of our personal universes than one which had to rotate around him or any of us.

In Luke 15, Jesus asks this question,

> *"Which one of you, having a hundred sheep and losing one*
> *of them, does not leave the ninety-nine in the wilderness and*
> *go after the one that is lost until he finds it?*

The answer, "None of us." If you leave nine sheep in the wilderness and go searching for the lost one, do you know how many sheep you'll have left. One if you find the lost one, likely, you'll lose them all. Crowds will always sacrifice the one to save the whole. In the crowd, there are no individuals, only herd. Consider the word *sheep*, which can mean one sheep, a flock of a hundred, every sheep on the planet, and every sheep that has ever existed. Flocks do not see the one. Jesus does. Contrary to our inability to see the individual and our willingness to sacrifice the individual for the whole, Jesus not only sees the single individual different from the flock, he seeks out the one. In John

10, Jesus describes himself as the shepherd who knows each sheep calling each one by name, valuing each as particular, distinct, and unique.

Consider these two parables from Jesus' teachings collected in the gospel of Matthew chapter 13,

> Jesus said, "The kingdom of heaven is like this. There was a treasure hidden in a field which someone discovered and hid, until he could go and sell everything he had and come back to purchase the whole field.
>
> "The kingdom of heaven is also like a merchant who searched tirelessly for fine pearls, and finding one of great value, he sold all he had and bought it."

A common approach to these parables is to put the hearer or reader in the role of seeker who finds the hidden Kingdom of God selling all he or she has to acquire it. Since God is usually the primary character in Jesus' parables, perhaps a better interpretation is seeing God as the one who finds the hidden treasure and the one who uncovers the hidden pearl. You are not the seeker – you are the one sought. You are not the finder – you are the one found. You are the treasure, lost in the earth, the sea, and at great cost, God seeks and finds you seeing you as what you are to God, the priceless treasure.

I cannot offer you value giving love in a book; I can only point to it. I believe that only God has the power and the maturity to give it to us consistently which is why Jesus constantly took time away from his family, his followers, and especially crowds to pray and reorient himself to the higher love he perceived from God. That's not just Jesus' story. It is your story. God has called you *Beloved*. The crowd will tell you otherwise, claiming to speak for God, claiming the ability to offer a valuation on people and groups like on a company in the stock market or cattle in an auction. The question for you is, whom will you believe: the crowd, or God?

Coming out of the crowd will be impossible for you if you are constantly looking to your crowds for validation, for affirmation, for appreciation, for approval, or for love. If you hope you can just be good enough, helpful enough, talented enough, powerful enough, forceful enough, attractive enough, or wealthy enough so that sooner or later people will accept you, value you, respect you, love you, then you will always be dependent on the crowd, lost in the herd, misplaced in the mass, and miss the treasure that you are. You will live looking for love in all the wrong places. You will always be longing for, hoping for, praying for some validation when, even if it comes, it won't last and will fall short of value giving love.

Yet, if you can open yourself to the voice of God, the blessing of God, the anointing of God, you can find a love that comes giving you what you tried to earn on your own. You will sense peace. And then, over time, learn to love in value giving ways that can celebrate the beauty in others because you see the beauty in yourself, the way God sees you. God becomes your mirror. When you look to God to see who you are, why would you need another source?

Living Loved

To step out of your crowd, to claim your place as beloved and valuable, takes tremendous courage like this woman in Mark chapter 5,

A large crowd was following Jesus, pressing in on him. In the midst of this mass was a woman who had been suffering from a bleeding disorder for a dozen years. She had endured the diagnosis of many physicians, spent all her money and resources on their cures, but had not gotten any better.

She had heard about Jesus and all he was doing in other places, so when he came near she tried to get to him, but the

crowd was in her way. After great effort, risking injury to herself, she got through the mob, and reached out and touched Jesus' coat.

Jesus stopped and asked, "Who touched me?"

The disciples, as on so many other occasions, could not understand Jesus' question. "What do you mean, who touched you?"

Jesus ignored them and looked around to see who had reached out to him. The woman was afraid of how he might react, but she also knew she was well. She fell down before him and told him everything.

Jesus spoke to her. He called her, "Daughter." He said, "Your faith has made you well. Go in peace. Be free from your disease."

Notice here, as in other places, the crowd seems to have a life of its own. The crowd is given a verb, they 'press' in on Jesus. If you feel like the group or groups you are part of are 'pressing' in on you, then you understand. This pressing may be physical, emotional, or mental.

Concerning the woman, the crowd does not notice her, but if it did, it would not have considered her worth their attention. By the laws of the day, she is substandard, unclean, a second-class status and a second-class gender. She is no person at all in the crowd because the crowd does not have persons but categories, which take away the identity of the individual. As Kierkegaard pointed out, "When you label me, you negate me." In the crowd, she is essentially invisible, even to Jesus' followers, lost and alone, not in the wilderness, but among the many.

The crowd is a physical and emotional barrier she must choose to face if she's going to get to Jesus. Oscar Wilde talked about the choice and the risk that goes with facing a crowd,

I won't tell you that the world (or the crowd) matters nothing, or the world's voice, or the voice of society. They matter a good deal. They matter far too much. But there are

moments when one has to choose between living one's own life, fully, entirely, completely—or dragging out some false, shallow, degrading existence that the world in its hypocrisy demands. You have that moment now. Choose!"

She chooses. She steps out. She risks. She moves through the mob the way a swimmer struggles in a stormy sea. She is determined and doesn't give up. She wants to get to Jesus. The contrast is vivid. The crowd is pressing and bumping, the woman is reaching and touching. The passage shows the connection of one person to another, a relating so powerful that even in the midst of a mob, both Jesus and the woman feel it.

"Who touched me?" Jesus asks. The disciples are unable to see a person in the mob. They ask, "How can you wonder who touched you? With the crowd packed so tightly together, how can you tell when one person ends and another begins?"

Even in the mass of people, Jesus is aware of a particular person, sensing her great need even in the midst of the mob's great passion. Jesus speaks to her. Addresses her. Jesus values her, esteems her, calls her, "Daughter."

Jesus understood he had a God-given value that was greater than any pseudo worth the crowd could try to give or deny, and she sensed it. She wanted to be more than the crowd, the doctors, the synagogue, the religious, and likely her own family told her she could be. She wanted to be well, physically, mentally, emotionally, and spiritually. She and Jesus exemplified love as individuals in the crowd, God's love embodied, giving and receiving, reaching out and being touched, blessing and being blessed. She is daughter of God as Jesus is Son. She is Beloved as Jesus is Beloved. This type of love does not come without risk, but the return is worth risking all.

The Family Crowd

Here is someone coming out of a crowd.
Can you guess who this is?

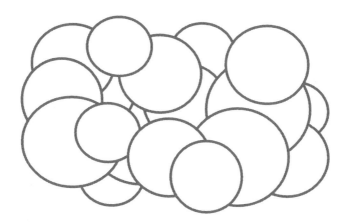

Maybe these additions will help.

Notice the familiar *S?* It's for Superman. Superman has some amazing abilities – *faster than a speeding bullet, more powerful than a locomotive, and able to leap tall buildings in a single bound!* My son and I, occasionally will pick superman's abilities and divide them among us. If I go first, I always pick flying. He picks super strength, something about out wrestling me.

Throughout the book, and specifically in this chapter, my purpose is not to show how you're superior to mere mortals, a swan living with ducks, or a wizard surrounded by muggles. My intent is to illustrate how all of us have our crowds, even Superman. We are all tigers pressured into goathood. Even the invincible Superman was silly putty in the conforming pressure of his two primary crowds:

Superman's Family Crowd

I don't mean the Kents from Kansas, but the family he came from on the planet Krypton. Every time a rock shows up from his past planet, he is as weak and frail as the infant he was before he left home. Something about his family of origin tears him up inside leaving him with no super powers at all. As seen in Superman, putting physical distance between ourselves and our families matters little if emotionally we are still fused together. Even if you move across the universe, wherever you go, there they are because there you are. As Madeline L'Engle said, "You are every age you've ever been."

Human development is cumulative. All your earlier ages and stages are still part of who you are. Like a building of multiple floors, just because you live at age fifty doesn't mean that age five isn't still inside.

We are especially tied to the ages when we experienced trauma. Trauma is simply any experience you don't have the mental capacity to categorize or comprehend. Even though you may rationalize such events, years later you may experience triggers which evoke in you that age, place, and experience all over again. For Superman, it was the explosion of his home planet. For natives to planet earth, we can each have different triggers that pull us back into the past, or pull the past to the present. Your triggers may be a phone call, a picture, a familiar setting or personal interaction that ties you back to an earlier stage. You can still have triggers no matter how healthy your family of origin, and if there was abuse, then the effect is magnified exponentially. The trauma you couldn't process then keeps coming back to you, exploding again and again. You are every age you've ever been.

Superman's Work Crowd or *The Daily Planet*

Superman dressed up as mild mannered Clark Kent so that he could get a job at a newspaper and write stories, often on the great things Superman was doing. His strategy was to belong by blending and taking on the persona of an average person. Through his false persona, he hoped others would accept him and that he could win the love of Lois Lane who could ultimately appreciate him for who he truly was by being who he wasn't. At first glance, a pair of glasses as a disguise should not fool anyone, but the glasses were only a small part of his masquerade. His persona was what fooled everyone. As Clark Kent, he became as bland as mashed potatoes. Even as a child reading the comic books, I wanted to yell at him, "You're Superman! Be Superman! You don't need a fake secret identity."

What would coming out of the crowd look like for Superman? Liberation. No longer would he be haunted by his childhood, the family from whence he came. Kryptonite would be just a green rock. It wouldn't make him feel like a powerless infant on an exploding planet.

Second, he wouldn't have to put on a fake identity. He could be Super Clark Kent. He could say, "Look, Lois, this is who I'm called to be. These are my gifts and what I must do. You can choose to be a part of it if you'd like." Who knows, maybe she had her own wonderful secret she was afraid to share. Regardless, the rest would be up to her, but it would stop the game that tormented his life.

What does coming out of the crowd look like for you? Simply, you don't have to be super, superior, successful, or even special, you just have to be particular. You can go and be wonderful, be amazing, fly if you can, but never because you have something to prove. Fly, fall, crawl, do it all, but because you're wonderful, valuable, and loved, not in hopes that one day you will be. You are accepted, and those who don't accept you can deal with it. Your quest is to discover, uncover, and grow the you-ness that makes you, you – the human you. Your calling is not to be super human, spectacular human, or even special human, but to be superbly human. Being human is challenge enough.

God doesn't seem to like repetition, so, even though crowds may act alike, dress alike, and try to conform you, blending you all in the name of unity, normalizing you into the casserole that is the crowd, you can still come apart. You can still live honestly, authentically, and as an individual, flying free from the gravity of crowds where you can think, choose, speak, and grow into the distinctive, unique person God intends for you to be and at the same time encourage others to do the same.

With Jesus, his family could have had the same infantizing control over him that Superman's family and kryptonite did over him. Jesus' family could have prevented him from maturing, from growing up, from living out his calling, but they didn't. He didn't let them. It doesn't mean they didn't try. Here is their attempt in Mark 3,

> *Jesus went back to his relatively quiet hometown and brought with him a wave of people filling the area. The town's people were saying, "What is the matter with Jesus? He is crazy! He has gone out of his mind!" When Jesus' family heard that Jesus had returned and all their neighbors were saying about him, they went out to restrain Jesus. Because of the crowd, they could not get to him. They waited outside and sent word into him, telling Jesus to come out so they could talk to him. Those nearest where Jesus was told him, "Your mother and your brothers are outside calling for you."*
>
> *Jesus replied, "My mother and brothers? Who are my mother and brothers?" He looked at those around him and said,*

"Here in front of me are my mother and brothers! Whoever does the will of God is my brother, sister, and mother."

Jesus' family did not come to support him, to get those in need of healing to line up, to try and keep the crowd from mobbing him, no, they came to restrain him, to tell him to quit stirring things up. The talk around town was that Jesus was arguing with the religious leaders of the day, he was breaking the Sabbath laws, he was making the scribes look bad, he was drawing so many people he might stir the punitive attention of Rome. His family was concerned that with all he was doing, he was going to get himself killed. (They were right about that.)

Jesus' family had become a crowd, and they tried to use their emotional power to reign in Jesus. They wanted him to conform to their expectations, their role, their calling. They were concerned about what their neighbors thought, about their family's reputation. Everyone was saying Jesus was crazy, and as a family, you want to save both your child and your family's reputation.

Likely, they could have gone inside to where Jesus was, and heard him as he talked to and taught the people in the crowd, but that was not their goal. They didn't want to hear what Jesus had to say, they had something to say to Jesus. They did not have a gift to bring, but a lecture to unload, and their intention was to let him have it! For such an encounter, they could not accomplish their mission in front of other people; they needed Jesus to come to them. The way many families speak to each other, at each other, is not meant to be heard in public, and so, they sent for him. "Have Jesus come out here so we can talk to him."

They sent for Jesus. Jesus didn't move. They commanded. He didn't respond. Contrary to the belief and desire of many families, the greatest honor you can do for your family is not to remain an infant going fetal like Superman exposed to kryptonite. The greatest honor that one can do for their family is to grow up with a story bigger than the one your family has for you, even if you have to resist the family to do it. For a child to grow up, parents have to grow up as well, and we need all the help we can get.

My friend Tommy has many temptations. One is hotdogs. The doctor told him, "Change your diet." Tommy did. Except for hotdogs. One day, Tommy went to Hardees not just for vice food but for comfort food. He was worried about his son's recent academic performance. He felt powerless to help him.

An older man came out of the restroom hallway, ordered, and then walked over to Tommy. "Can I sit with you?"

Tommy looked around. No one else in the restaurant, yet, with all those places to sit, he said to Tommy, "Can I sit with you?"

"Okay," Tommy said.

The man was a talker, a retired teacher, a tutor. Tommy would reflect later, "There I was complaining to God when along comes a tutor, someone who had been helping students for years."

The tutor told Tommy, "Give your son some space. Don't come down on his every move. You are over worrying about him. If you're breathing down his neck, then he can't see what his choices are. Your son is trying to grow up, make sure you don't get in his way. Help, don't hinder."

But we do hinder, all in the name of love, and safety. No parents want to see their child experience pain. It hurts us far too much. Even in the comic book, Superman's parents sent him into space not so he could be amazing; they just wanted him to live. As "good" parents, we keep our children from getting hurt, a role we never give up no matter how old our children become. Generally, parents seldom mature without help from their children.

Jesus was aware of what most of us seem to miss, besides being loving and nurturing, families can be quite dangerous to our health and growth. As Barbara Sher noted,

How can families harm us when they love us? Very easily, unfortunately. Most of us overlook one important fact when we think love is enough: Love and respect aren't the same thing.

Love is fusion. As a baby, you belong to your parents, you're extension of them. Respect is differentiation: you belong to yourself, and you're an extension of no one. Differentiation is essential for happiness of adults.

When we pray for, bless, or baptize babies in churches, I think we do a disservice to families. The idea the church will help you 'nurture and raise your son or daughter in the Christian faith' seems so supportive. There should be a disclaimer. God has a greater vision for each child than the often-restricting dreams, visions, and plans parents, pastors, teachers, and others will offer.

Jesus had a bigger story than his family's story for him. It was God's story. He invited others, including his family to come along, to grow with him, and he called others out of their family crowds to do the same. If you do not have a story bigger than your family's story for you, you will keep going back to them for approval. Smothered by your family crowd, you will likely never mature past the most mature person in the family, and most of the time you will spend catering to the most immature, taking on whatever roles the family has for you in an ever repeating drama. The best help you can give your family is to have a calling greater than the role you play in your family. For example, consider what Jesus did for Peter. When Peter encountered Jesus, not only was it life changing, it was name changing. John 1 has Jesus saying to him, "You've been called Simon (which means 'sand'), but from now on you'll be known as Peter (which means 'rock'.)" Peter's family thought enough of him to name him, "Sand," but Jesus had a bigger vision for him than his family, and to show it, he called him, "Rock." Without a greater calling, like Simon, we will just continue to be sand blown about by our crowds.

The Universal Crowd

One of my favorite routines by Bill Cosby was on *The Tonight Show* back when Johnny Carson hosted. It went something like this...

When George Washington was a little boy, his father gave him a new hatchet. When playng by himself, he took his little hatchet and chopped down his father's favorite cherry tree. Upon finding the tree, George's father came and asked him, "George, did you cut down my cherry tree?"

George replied, "Father, I cannot tell a lie. I cut it down with me little hatchet."

Do you think George's father punished him? Of course he did. His father didn't know that he was THE George Washington.

Thomas Alva Edison growing up was a curious boy. He once burned down the family barn because he wanted to see what would happen in a fire that large. Do you think his father punished him? Of course he did. He didn't know that he was THE Thomas Alva Edison.

Mark Twain pushed over an outhouse that fell down a hill and into the Mississippi River. Do you think his mother punished him? Of course she did. She was in the outhouse when he pushed it over. And she didn't know he was THE Mark Twain.

Just to be alive, you are THE you. Rabbi Nachman of Bratzlav expressed our particularity as God's design, "God never does the same thing twice." Martin Buber takes this idea a step further when he says, "Uniqueness is the essential good of persons that each is given to unfold." You are unique and have a unique responsibility to grow in distinctiveness that is THE you.

People of all faiths should celebrate the beauty of the particularity of life, of all life, and of each life, particularly each person. To help us celebrate life, Charles Darwin presented the church with a beautiful gift. However, as with Galileo, the church rejected Darwin's gift and marked it with a huge, *Return to Sender*. The majority of religious leaders and religious people in Darwin's day and since have wanted little of Darwin's gift.

In a counter argument to Darwin, William Paley, a physician and a theologian, looked at the world and its complexity and offered this illustration as proof that the world didn't evolve over time but was produced, as is, by God.

Imagine you're walking down the beach and your foot hits a rock. You probably won't wonder, "Where did that rock come from?" because you don't expect an interesting answer to that question. Maybe it was always there. Maybe it fell from the sky. But suppose you are walking on the beach and found a watch on the ground and then you asked where the watch had come from.

Paley pointed out that, unlike a rock washed ashore, complex machines like watches don't just appear on beaches. Machines need a maker. To believe the watch just happened would be foolish, and so he cited Darwin's ideas as foolish. In a more contemporary example, the argument against Darwin's observations is to imagine a tornado blows through a junkyard and the result is not chaos but a huge airplane. Chaos does not lead to complexity but needs a craftsman, an engineer, with an intelligent design.

The problem with these metaphors is that they are mechanical. Paley pointed to an industrial model of the universe. Darwin pointed at an organic one. To view the world as a machine misses Darwin's insight altogether and the beauty of life.

Alan Watts challenged the industrial image that God "made" the world. The rules for production in factories are far different from the principles that apply to life. Watts pointed out that with a mechanical model is a common way of thinking in Western culture,

> It is perfectly natural in our culture for a child to ask its mother 'How was I made?' or 'Who made me?' And this is a very, very powerful idea, but for example, it is not shared by the Chinese, or by the Hindus. A Chinese child would not ask its mother 'How was I made?' A Chinese child might ask its mother 'How did I grow?' which is an entirely different procedure from making. You see, when you make something, you put it together, you arrange parts, or you work from the outside in, as a sculptor works on stone, or as a potter works on clay. But when you watch something growing, it works in exactly the opposite direction. It works from the inside to the outside. It expands. It burgeons. It blossoms. And it happens all of itself at once. In other words, the original simple form, say of a living cell in the womb, progressively complicates itself, and that's the growing process, and it's quite different from the making process.

Watts used this image and said that if you look at an apple tree it is not a factory for apples, it does not produce apples, it apples. In the same way an apple tree apples, a giraffe giraffes, and the world peoples. Life produces life, and that life is not a factory reproduction of an engineered design, but each beautiful in unique characteristics.

This is not Christianity vs. Hinduism, or Creation vs. Evolution, or even America vs. China. It is a mechanical model compared to an organic model. With the exception of a potter, the majority references in the Bible have God working in an organic rather than factory way. In the beginning, according to Genesis 1, God creates time and life, and sets them working together in a wonderful rhythm of day and night. Genesis 1,

> And God said, "Let the waters bring forth swarms of living creatures, and let birds fly above the earth across the dome of the sky.
>
> God imparts life to the seas, and they bring forth life. The same paradigm is orchestrated with the land.
>
> And God said, "Let the earth bring forth living creatures of every kind: cattle and creeping things and wild animals of the earth of every kind.
>
> Then God creates humanity in God's image and charges us with life,
>
> "Be fruitful and multiply."

Instead of reading the first chapter of Genesis as insight to God's life factory, the scripture, like the science of Darwin, points to the beauty and rhythm of life. Rabbi Abraham Joshua Heschel stated,

> The Biblical words about the genesis of heaven and earth are not words of information but words of appreciation. The story of creation is not a description of how the world came into being but a song about the glory of the world's having come into being. "And God saw that it was good."

The response of the living is to live, not to prove we are alive, or justify our existence, or even to proclaim how or what God exactly did in creation but instead focus on the particular gift of life that is in each person. The fundamentalists and the physicists agree, in the history of the world, THE me, THE you, and THE others that we meet each day are here, alive, beautiful, and wonderful in a unique distinctiveness that belongs to each person. In each life comes a responsibility to live each life fully. Howard Thurman cited living fully as both our central task and the hope for the world. Thurman said,

> If you want to change the world, discover what makes you fully alive because what the world needs are people that are fully alive.

When it comes to products, we can speak in universals and uniformity, all those watches by a certain watchmaker are relatively identical. Darwin's gift was to approach all differences with curiosity and wonder. If we can learn this approach, then what a wonderful world it will be.

We have three children, two daughters and a son, and none are alike. Each so dynamically different that we are constantly reminded that if we are going to help them grow, we have to continually adapt how we are with each of them respecting each personality, each soul among us. And if we forget, they remind us. I would never say to one of them, "You are so like your sister," anymore than I would say to my wife, "You are just like your mother." Either comment would show that I just don't get it.

When I forget the distinct personality, the particular possibility and potential each has, they remind me, like when my son, Nathan, showed me the possibilities of a trashcan when seen through his eyes. For me, the trashcan in my office had one purpose and no other. Then Nathan and I were waiting on his sisters and with a half hour of creativity before us. Nathan started inventing games and the trashcan transformed before me. It became a stool, a storage container, a hurdle, a hat, a drum, and of course, a paper wad basketball goal. Because Nathan is alive he can envision, name, and make more than trashcans, he can make possibilities. He is possibility in a unique and distinctive way that is his and his alone.

To be a product is to be uniform, universal, and interchangeable. To be alive is to be unique. No child was made like a watch, car, or airplane. No child is a factory model.

Sigmund Freud's basic assumption still shapes modern psychology. Our models of human development still assume that each of us is naturally an individual ignoring that we are each born into our families, communities, and cultures and to grow into a particular person is our life-long task and the central requirement for living in healthy relationship with others as Rabbi Heschel counseled,

> *You can only sense a person if you are a person. Being a person depends upon being alive to the wonder and mystery that surrounds us, upon the realization that there is no ordinary person.*

The role of parents, teachers, leaders, and all adults is to enable children to celebrate their particular individuality and personhood as well as that of other persons. Educator Ken Robinson tells about an interview he conducted with Gillian Lynne, choreographer for *Cats*, *Phantom of the Opera*, and other famous musicals. Robinson asked her how she got to be a dancer. She said that when she was in school, in the 1930's, the school wrote to her parents and said, "We think Gillian has a learning disorder." Her mother took her to see a specialist. Gillian sat on her hands and tried to hold still while her mother talked to a doctor about all the problems Gillian was having at school, how she was disturbing other students, how her homework was always late, on and on her mother chattered. When her mother finished talking, the doctor went over, sat next to Gillian, and spoke to her. He said, "Gillian, I've listened to all these things your mother told me, and I need to talk to her in private. Wait here. We'll be back soon. It won't take long."

The doctor escorted her mother out of the room, but before he left, he turned on the radio. As soon as they were out of the office, Gillian was up and  moving to the music. The doctor and her mother watched from the hallway. After a few minutes the doctor said, "Mrs. Lynne, Gillian isn't sick. She's a dancer. Take her to dance school." She did, and Gillian described going to dance school like this, "We walked in this room and it was full of people like me – people who couldn't sit still; people who had to move to think." She grew to become part of the Royal Ballet, work with Andrew Lloyd Weber, and give delight to the imaginations of millions. Fortunately, the doctor, when she was eight didn't put her on medication and tell her to sit still. Apparently, that doctor saw her potential and knew that she was THE Gillian Lynne long before she, or her mother, or anyone else did.

Likely, even if your family or your groups know you're THE you, they may forget. Patiently remind them, but don't require them to see it before you claim it for yourself and help others do the same. Be Beloved. Be beautiful. Be THE you God created you to be. And then, like the doctor did for Gillian Lynne, go around helping others celebrate the beauty of each particular life.

The Competitive Crowd

What popular British television show is represented in the following picture?

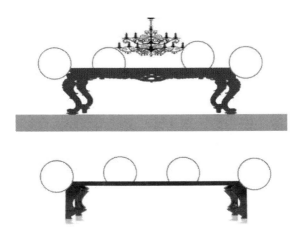

The show is *Downton Abbey*. At Downton, there is a clear ranking in the upstairs and the downstairs tables. The Lords and Ladies of the estate sit upstairs. They eat assisted by the servants. When they are not on duty, the servants eat at their table downstairs. The different floors give a visual hierarchy to the rank of the family and the servant classes. Each table also has a hierarchy ranking each space around the table. Upstairs, the Lord of the house is in the seat of honor. Downstairs, it is the head butler. The cook's helper doesn't even get a seat at the servants' table but has to eat in the kitchen.

Here is a numerical ranking with 1 for the head of the table and 2 is the seat to the right and 3 to the left.

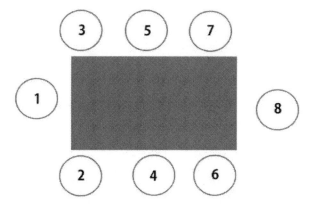

Growing up, as the youngest of four, I understood hierarchical tables. Every Thanksgiving, I had to sit at a card table out of sight of the dining room and its majestically set out feast. In junior. high and high school, I learned more about table hierarchies. Everyone sat with his or her group. To cross the divide between tables would have been as out of place as for a servant from downstairs Downton Abbey to ascend to the upper table and take a seat.

Post-graduation, I learned about rankings on corporate ladders where the higher you go the better your pay and place in society. I even found a hierarchical ranking in my neighbourhood. We have a nice house. I like it. It is brick on the front and siding around the back. I felt good about it until I noticed the houses in the subdivision higher up the hill. Those houses are all brick. Ascend even higher up the hill and if you know the gate's password, you'll find even larger and nicer houses.

As long as there have been groupings of people, there have been hierarchies to tell us who we are and how we rank as well as where we can sit and where we can't. Jesus' era was no different. In this passage, Jesus went to a dinner party where the seating arrangement was unclear in Luke 14,

Jesus went to a leader's home for dinner. The religious officials were watching Jesus closely. Jesus was also watching

them. He noticed how they were jockeying for position around the dinner table for the places of honor so he told them this parable,

"When you are invited by someone to a wedding banquet, don't sit down at the place of honor. Someone more distinguished in the community than you are might come. Then the host of the party will come and ask you to move. All the other seats will be taken and you'll have to do the walk of shame to the far end of the table and take the lowest seat. Instead, take the lowest seat when you arrive, then the host will come along and say, 'What are you doing here? You should be nearer to the head of the table.' Then you will do the walk of honor in front of all as the host will escort you to a higher place."

He summed up the parable and said, "Those who exalt themselves will be humbled, and those who humble themselves will be exalted."

In this passage, Jesus is attending a wedding. The guests are navigating the room for position in the table top twenty. Jesus advises them, "Don't choose the higher ranking seats at the table, or else someone will come and move you lower. Instead, take the lower seat, and then someone will come along and raise you up. Take my advice, exalt yourself and you'll be humbled. Humble yourself, and you will be exalted."

In the two thousand years since Jesus gave this counsel, many people have taken the lower seat, accepted the downstairs table, and are still waiting for someone to come along and lift them up to a higher place. I'm not saying that Jesus is wrong. Jesus is intentionally being absurd, and he knows it. The problem is, we don't. We don't see the charade because we believe in the table and the table hierarchies to tell us our place, to inform us who we are relative to others and what our value is in the world.

Rather than debate whether or not Jesus is giving an intentional farce, just try his advice. Go to a professional football game during the playoffs. Buy tickets for seats on the fifty-yard line, but instead of sitting there, go and find someone who has a ticket for the worst possible seat in the stadium and trade with them. See if anyone comes to raise you back to the seat you deserve, the one you purchased. See if the beer guy comes around and says, "Hey! What are you doing here? You shouldn't be up here. You belong on the fifty yard line." He won't. He'll just say, "Bud Light? Miller Light? Peanuts?" He won't care where you are sitting.

"Take the lower seat and someone will raise you up?" That's not the way the world works. Jesus knows it. If you're paying attention, you know it, too. Think about those who humble themselves in service of our communities. Consider public school teachers. They are some of the smartest people among us doing one of the greatest services to our country. Today, they are asked to not only teach children but to help parent them as well. Are they exalted? No, look at their pay checks. Ask a teacher if she or he will one day be raised up to places of corporate honor. They'll laugh at you.

Consider nurses. A skilled nurse can be as helpful an aid to healing as a doctor. They perform services to the ill most of us shudder in considering, but they are not raised up in honor. What about the school and hospital custodians? Those institutions could not function without them. Consider parents who stay home for the welfare of the children in the family. It's hard work, but you can't put it on a job resume. Humble yourself and you will be exalted? Not going to happen. Jesus knows it, and so does the writer of the gospel, which is why this piece of advice on how to live comes with a wink. The wink is when the writer says, "He told them this parable..." The moral instruction is not instruction at all. It is a parable. Parables are parallels, one thing set alongside another. Once we set Jesus' advice parallel to life as we experience it, then we realize that we pulled into a gas station, asked for directions, and Jesus purposely sent us down a dead end street. If you take Jesus' advice, take the low seat so that you will be raised up, you'll only be frustrated. That's Jesus' hope. Jesus is not trying to fool anyone. We are already fooled. Jesus is not telling what he hopes people will believe. He is saying what we've already bought into – that we are our seat at the table, our class rank, our bank account, our partially bricked homes, or our place on the corporate ladder. He is not trying to get us to believe that if we take a low seat someone will raise us up; he is pointing to the absurdity of the whole system. Jesus sent us trying to figure out the table ranking system not as a guaranteed way of success but a sure-fire path to failure. Only when the ladder of success crumbles do we consider that perhaps we had been climbing the wrong wall. Hopefully, then we can transcend the ridiculous seating charts and all other ranking systems. Jesus did. So have others.

In *The Art of Possiblity*, Boston Symphony Conductor Benjamin Zander tells about his childhood family table. He was the youngest of four with two older brothers and an older sister. Every evening at dinnertime, they would sit around the table, with the parents in the places of authority at the ends and the kids in the middle. Ben's dad would begin the conversation by addressing the oldest boy, "What did you do today?"

Ben's brother would describe, at some length all he had accomplished. Ben understood that "What did you do today?" meant, "What did you achieve today? How did you bring glory and honor to the family? How were you successful?"

Then Ben's father would ask the second in line, his other brother, "What did you do today?" and he would relate all his accomplishments. Then his sister. Then Ben. Ben felt, compared to his older siblings, he accomplished little. No matter what he had achieved, one of his siblings had done it before and done it better.

As an adult looking back on his childhood, he realized that his family dinner table with the nightly tabulation of daily scores was simply a competitive game between brothers and sister, between his family and the world. Even though it seemed like the ultimate measurement of his worth, or lack of worth, it was simply a game. Once he realized it was not real but a game, he transcended it. He realized he could choose his own way in the world, how he lived, and the table environment he wanted to give to his children. He chose not to imitate the scoring and seating of the broader culture, but instead to choose differently.

Zander chose to create a different table for his family with a different set of rules and a different central question. Instead of asking "What did you do today?" or "How did you compete today?" Zander asked his family, "What did you contribute today?", "What did you give?", and, "How did you make someone's day better?"

As a symphonic conductor, Zander realized that it was not just who got first chair in each section that made for a great symphony but from having every member of the orchestra contributing to his or her fullest potential. For his family, the guideline was the same. His role as parent was to help his children learn what each had to contribute, seeing themselves as contributors with something to offer, with gifts the world needs.

The beauty of Jesus as he stood before the measuring table at the home of a Pharisee was that the table had no claim on him. Wherever Jesus sat was the head of the table. There was no ladder, pyramid, or ruler to measure Jesus. He was beautiful. His life was art. He had something to give. He was the gift. Instead of vying for position at someone else's table, he set a table for others. Everywhere he went he was setting a place mat down for others and pulling out a chair saying, "There is a place for you in this world. You have something to contribute."

The Career Crowd

When Jesus calls the first disciples, he calls them from not just their families, but out of their jobs and careers and into a vocation. The distinction between these three is significant and can be seen in Mark 1,

> *Jesus was walking along the Sea of Galilee, where he saw Simon and his brother Andrew, who were fishermen, casting nets into the lake.*
>
> *Jesus speaks to them, "Follow me, and I will make you fishers of people." And immediately, they left their nets and followed him.*
>
> *In a similar matter, after walking on a little farther, Jesus, now with Simon and Andrew tagging along, calls out to James and John who were in their family boat with their father, Zebedee. Like the two before, then immediately left their nets, their boat, and their father, and followed Jesus.*

In this passage are three groups: the hired men, the fishermen, and the disciples or followers of Jesus. They illustrate the three different ways we work: jobs, careers, and vocations.

JOBS

A job involves basic skill, basic labor, and basic pay to try and meet basic needs. In the passage, these are the workers, those on Zebedee's boat who likely did a day's work for a day's pay.

My first job was in a textile mill in South Carolina when I was sixteen. I worked second shift, from 4:00 to midnight. I learned to drink coffee dispensed nightly for a quarter out of a vending machine and was paid by the hour.

CAREERS

A career differs from a job in training and role. A career has background, education, experience, and investment. Jesus encountered some career fishermen in Zebedee and sons with their boat. They had training, skill, and investment in the family business.

After college, I went to seminary, twice. I earned masters degrees in youth ministry and divinity. I studied Greek and Hebrew and passed ordination exams. This is my career, accepted into the Presbyterian system, ordained, blessed, and allowed to pastor. I even have a pension. Do you think Andrew or Simon asked Jesus if he had a health plan or a pension program before dropping their nets at the shore? Likely not.

The word, "career," comes from the Latin word for *car,* which comes from *carrera,* which means "racetrack." Like a racetrack, careers have structure, direction, and competition. And, like a  racetrack, a career can have you feeling like you are going very fast, around, and around, in circles, never ending. No matter who wins a particular race, another competition will start shortly, and another, and another. And if you cannot fill your lane, don't worry, there will be another to take your place and the race will keep moving, and moving, and moving.

Students are set on college tracks and career tracks taught to compete with each other in race after race, score after score. Students are ranked, from first to last, high to low, with their cumulative score or grade point average. We score their schools as well. The hope is to prepare students to take their place in society and to keep racing as our economy depends on it. They are promised great rewards for their effort, and if they work hard enough and succeed, they can drink from the cup of glory, whatever that is.

Kierkegaard warned about the effects of our jobs and careers and the responsibility of communities to watch out for each other in this story,

> *A farm village's crop was infested by a strange bug that contaminated all their food. Once they realized that eating the food made them crazy, they quit eating it. Then they started to starve. The village leaders met and agreed they must eat to survive, but they also decided to work together to remind each other that the very food they ate to survive made them crazy.*

Taking our place in crowds, pursuing careers, doing all that we do for food, family, groups, culture, is dangerous when we forget the madness that they can produce, then around and around we go, faster and faster and call it life, saying, "We have no choice."

When you live going only in circles, how can a sense of direction be possible? The church should be that village voice, the agreement upon leaders that the very food that we eat makes us mad, calling the crowds into question, challenging our consumer economy, our chasing the dollar. We should join the prophets, poets, and playwrights, like Charles Bukowski,

> *Some lose all mind*
> *and become soul, insane*
> *some lose all soul*
> *and become mind, intellectual*
> *some lose both*
> *and become accepted.*

In a critique of business life in America, Arthur Miller wrote *The Death of a Salesman*. Willy Loman, the tragic character who dominates the play, is laid to rest in a cemetery following his suicide. At the graveside on a bleak and rainy day, the immediate family is huddled together along with a couple of friends. His wife cries softly over the casket, "Why? Why? Why did you do it, Willy?" It is then that Willy's son, Biff, speaks and says, "Aw, shucks, Mom. Aw, shucks. He had all the wrong dreams. He had all the wrong dreams."

VOCATION

When I read or tell of the calling of the disciples, I am often asked, "How could they just leave everything – job, career, family, and follow Jesus with no more information, and no guarantees?"

My question is, "How could they not?" James, John, Simon, and Andrew weren't very good fishermen, we have record of them fishing all night and not catching anything on more than one occasion, and they seldom seem to be fishing but are instead always fixing their boat or mending their nets. But there is more, besides giving them an out to a career they seem ill suited for, Jesus gave them their calling, their *vocatio*. "Vocation" comes from the Latin word, *vocare,* which means, "to call." Carl Jung describes people with vocation,

> *What is it, in the end, that induces someone to go his own way and to rise out of unconscious identity with the mass as out of a swathing mist? Not necessity, for necessity comes to many, and they all take refuge in convention. Not moral decision, for nine times out of ten we decide for convention likewise. What is it, then, that inexorably tips the scales in favor of the extra-ordinary?*
>
> *It is what is commonly called vocation: an irrational factor that destines a person to emancipate himself from the herd and from its well-worn paths.*

Vocation is not for God to hear you calling, but for you to hear God's calling. Vocation is not for God to respond to the desires of your heart but for you to align your life with the passion and fire

60

of God's heart. Vocation is not for you to have a five-year plan that makes sense to you but for you to live in a way that makes sense to God. To align your life with the heart of God, to live Jesus' way in the world, to discover your distinctive and particular place as an alive human in the image of God will give purpose and meaning to your life, Frederick Buechner said, "

> *The vocation for you is the one in which your deep gladness and the world's deep need meet – something that not only makes you happy but that the world needs to have done.*

Vocation is both self-fulfilling and world fulfilling. It is both living into your calling of becoming not just a beloved child of God, but a beloved adult of God and facilitating the world's growth into The Kingdom of God, which Jesus illustrated in Matthew 5 with the following imagery,

> *Each of you is the salt of the earth. If salt has no flavor, can you make it salty again? No, unless it gives flavor to food, it's thrown out and trampled on.*
>
> *Each of you is the light of the world. When people get together and build a city, they don't hide it in a valley but put it on a hill so others can come to it. In the same way, why would anyone light a candle or a lamp and put it under a bucket? No, you put it on the table so that it gives light to all the house.*
>
> *So let it be with you. Let your light shine so that others may see the wonder of what you do and give glory*

Being flavor for the earth, letting our light shine, stepping out like a city on a hill, or a singer on stage, can take great courage, bravery that often takes years to develop.

One of my dearest friends is Etta Britt. She got her first 'record deal' a little older than the Nashville norm. Here is a selection of an article by Lori Weiss in *The Huffington Post* on Etta's story, *It Ain't Over – Out of the Shadows, Mom Signs Record Deal at 55*

From the time Etta Britt was a young girl, she was singing back-up for Diana Ross. It's just that Diana didn't know it. Because Etta was in front of her bedroom mirror in Louisville, Kentucky -- hair brush in hand, as a microphone, of course -- pretending she was one of the Supremes.

"I'd stand there for hours," Etta laughed, "and pretend I was on stage. And my brother would come in and tease me, and I'd throw the hairbrush at him."

"When I walk out on stage, I often say 'You're probably wondering who I am. Well, I'm a 55-year-old woman who just got her first record deal.' And I get a standing ovation.

"Just like the title of the CD, I feel like I'm coming out of the shadows," Etta said with a tear in her eye. "And now I'm showing my daughters that it doesn't matter what your age is -- you can still make your dreams come true."

Etta came out of her shadows, her cultural, familial, and her own mental crowd to let her light shine. She celebrated the voice she had to share and the songs she has to sing, and encourages others to do the same. When you step out like Etta, it gives other people encouragement to come out of their own shadows and let their light shine. If you get the chance to watch a singer like Etta, one who is a band leader as well as a performer, one who is an encourager sharing both her light and the spotlight, sharing her music and weaving together the music of others, then you can see how one soul taking her place encourages others to do the same.

Etta and I have found these words by Author Marianne Williamson encouraging in both coming out of the shadows and the crowd,

Our deepest fear is not that we are inadequate,
Our deepest fear is that we are powerful
beyond measure.
It is our light, not our darkness, that most frightens us.
We ask ourselves, who am I to be?
Who are you not to be?

You are a child of God.
Your playing small doesn't serve the world.
There is nothing enlightened about shrinking
so that other people won't feel insecure around you.
We were born to make manifest
the glory of God within us.
It is not just in some of us: it is in (all of us),
And as we let our own light shine,
we unconsciously give other people
permission to do the same.

The Two Christmases Crowd

This one should be easy. What jolly ol' elf is this?

Of course, it's Santa.

Standing in line, list in hand, waiting to buy a friend, relative, spouse, or child a gift even though he, she, they already have materially far more than they need. Waiting for the cashier, as she swipes the credit card of the person in front of us, many feel something inside stir, which says, "Something about this is terribly wrong." All across the world, we feel and see the discrepancy between Jesus and the way we 'celebrate' his birth. Yet, we go along. We have two Christmases. One we call Christmas and the other we call Christmas, which makes it even more confusing. Keeping the two Christmases separate is both challenging and perplexing as Author Augusten Burroughs points out,

> *As a young child I had Santa and Jesus all mixed up. I could identify Coke or Pepsi with just one sip, but I could not tell you for sure why they strapped Santa to a cross. Had he missed a house? Had a good little girl somewhere in the world not received the doll he'd promised her, making the father angry?"*

Even as a pastor, during worship, I can't always tell which of the two Christmases I'm celebrating – the one with angels bringing "good news for all people," or one with the giant "to-do", "to decorate", and "to order by December 23rd" lists.

Three Sundays prior to Jesus' birthday, I visited a church for their Sunday worship. For the anthem, a singer stepped out to the middle of the worship space and sang a marvellous rendition of The Christmas Song, which, of course, has nothing about Jesus but does have some nice lyrics in praise of Santa,

Tiny tots with their eyes all aglow
Will find it hard to sleep tonight
They know that Santa's on his way
He's loaded lots of toys and goodies on his sleigh.
And every mother's child is gonna spy
To see if reindeer really know how to fly

The crowd, I mean congregation, applauded. Offended, I almost walked out. I would have left, but I had friends with me. I did not want to have to explain why I left. I also had nowhere else to go. I did make a vow that no worship service I led to the Glory of God in celebration of the birth of Jesus would ever have such a pagan song in it.

I kept my promise for two weeks. The Sunday before Jesus' birthday, we were holding a worship service on a farm. A family came who had not been to many church activities since their children had been born. We were glad to have them. As we gathered in our circle, we sang some very appropriate Christmas songs, and finally, to prepare our hearts and minds for the sermon, Etta, our worship leader, asked, "Anyone have any other Christmas songs you'd like to sing?"

The answer was, from a five year old, Rudolf The Green Nosed Reindeer. Even though I was certain I was going to hell for it, here was this child who hadn't been to church often, no one had explained to her about our two Christmases, and we wanted her to feel connected, so we sang Rudolf The Green Nosed Reindeer. Yes, I know, most versions have Rudolf with a red nose, but we sang it like that, and likely will for years to come.

The blending between the two Christmases is tough. I'm not about to have Santa skip my house. I don't think there is a rational argument that any adult can give a child why a non-commercial Christmas is better for everyone.

The hardest crowd to overcome is the cultural one, especially this one with the two Christmases. It is worldwide and now includes 'crowd' in the definition. The origin of the term Christmas came from Christ Mass which meant the worship (Mass) in celebration of the coming of Christ. Now it takes the more common definition of mass which as an adjective means, relating to a large body of people. For example, The movie has mass appeal. Is there a holiday with more mass appeal than Christmas? Is there a larger crowd across the world than those who 'celebrate' Christmas? (You know which one I mean.)

To come out of this crowd would be quite difficult. To call the Christmas that has little to do with Jesus superficial and shallow but then do nothing for Jesus' birthday would be Scroogeish. Not only would your children attack you while you slept but ghosts of Christmases past, present, and future would haunt you for all twelve days of Christmas.

I know the difference between Christmas and Christmas. I have the freedom to choose differently. The pressure to conform is not just from current culture but almost fifty years of personal Christmases. If any of my children said to me, "I don't want Christmas gifts this year. I think we should do something else with the money." Part of me would rejoice, yet, deep inside, I would ask, "What about Christmas? Can't we just send some money to Heifer International and buy somebody a goat so we don't feel guilty?"

So, we just accept it. We celebrate two Christmases and are glad we don't have to pick between them. Which would you rather have, a Christmas without a nativity or a Christmas without presents? We pick both, afraid of what we would choose. We blend the music, even the symbols, with Santa at the nativity or even holding an infant Christ with a halo. We remember Jesus, go to church, read the Christmas story (the one with the angels, not the one where soldiers kill babies), and then, all the rest of our focus goes to making our lists and checking them twice.

There is nothing in the Bible against Christmas. Jesus didn't say anything about not having two Christmases. He did say this, Luke 16,

> *It is impossible for a slave to serve two masters; for a slave will either hate the one and love the other, or be devoted to the one and despise the other. In the same way, you cannot serve God and money or wealth.*

Sure we have our two Christmases, but we glorify and worship Jesus. We use currency, but our faith and ultimate trust is in God, it says so right on our money. Clearly, we have two  Christmases, but don't we also have two currencies? In Luke 12, Jesus seems to present another either/or in regards to money,

> *Sell all your possessions and give them away. Make purses and wallets for yourselves that don't wear out with an unfailing treasure in heaven, where no thief comes near and no moth can destroy. Wherever your treasure is, there your heart will be.*

We are just as content with two currencies as we are with two Christmases. We will take our spending frenzy and hold out for Jesus' birthday, and then we will pretend our love of money is an act of faith as we blur the two. How do we not notice the similarity in language we use about churches and money? We have denominations of money and of churches. We speak of Jesus paying our debts. We talk about people as if they are currency asking, "How many members do you have?" which sounds similar to, "How much money do you have?" We even use the same adjective to describe God. We pray to the Almighty God while we chase after the Almighty Dollar. Aren't a significant percentage of our prayers dollar related?

We have also transformed the call of God to a call on God. Prayer has become formulaic as we turn our wish lists for ourselves, those we care about, and the world over to God throughout the year. We go to church for the 'secrets of prayer.' The opening to a bestselling book by a bestselling preacher begins,

I heard a story about a man on vacation in Hawaii with his wife. He was a good man who had achieved a modest measure of success, but he was coasting along, thinking that he'd already reached his limits in life. One day, a friend was driving the couple around the island, showing them the sights. They stopped to admire a gorgeous house set high on a hill. The property was replete with beautiful palm trees and lush green gardens in a picturesque, peaceful setting with a panoramic view overlooking the ocean.

As the man gazed at the magnificent home, he commented to his wife and friend, "I can't even imagine living in a place like that."

Right there, something inside him said, 'Don't worry. You won't. You will never live in a great place like that.'

Startled at his own thoughts, he asked himself, 'What do you mean?'

As long as you can't imagine it, as long as you can't see it, then it is not going to happen for you. The man correctly realized that his own thoughts and attitudes were condemning him to mediocrity. He determined then and there to start believing better of himself, and believing better of God.

It's the same way with us. We have to conceive it on the inside before we're ever going to receive it on the outside.

Try this exercise. Go through the Bible, and at each invasive place where God shows up, substitute God's goal with –*a beach house in Hawaii.*

For example, God speaks to Moses at the burning bush, "I've heard the cries of my people in slavery under the injustice of Pharaoh, and I've come down to... *give you a beach house in Hawaii.*" Changes the story altogether, doesn't it?

God speaks to Jonah, "I've seen the evil of the people of Nineveh, so go, I'm sending you to...*my beach house in Hawaii.*"

The Angel Gabriel appears to Mary, "Blessed art thou among women for God has chosen you *to receive a beach house in Hawaii.*" "How can this be?" Mary responds. "Since I have no credit?"

Imagine Jesus, in the call to discipleship, "If anyone would come after me, let them deny themselves, pick up their cross, and follow me *to my beach house in Hawaii.*"

There are so many Bible versions out there today, where can I find that one? Churches that promise, "Prayer is the way to open God's storehouse of the blessings God has for you," will certainly draw a crowd, television sponsorship, lots of money, and if no one else gets a beach house in Hawaii, at least the pastors can have one. Somebody has to. Nice work if you can get it.

As adults, we want God to do for us what we wanted Santa to do for us as kids. Is this way of believing different from the one we held as children in December?

We really aren't interested in two Christmases or two currencies, only one, the one we give our hearts to, the one we look to in order to make us and our children happy, the one that symbolizes where we believe our dreams can be fulfilled. Our society encourages us to go on a spending bender all in the name of Jesus, for his birthday. We talk about the Exodus story of Israel's infidelity with a golden calf but see no correlation to a giant bull on Wall Street. Do we have any dreams as individuals, as communities, as nations not dependent on money and the economy, that don't ultimately see the dollar and not God as almighty? Isn't this the reason faith in Jesus has become a mental exercise of memorizing creed, catechism, or selected passages of scripture so we can believe in him but put our trust elsewhere? We go along with the crowd, but do so in Jesus' name. If we are honest with ourselves, do we hope for and work toward any dreams that don't have a price tag on them? Isn't money the path to making our dreams come true? If so, haven't we then put a price tag on our souls? Jesus warns in Luke 9,

What will it profit you if you get all you wish for, including the whole world, but it cost you your soul?

It is not God we are fooling, but ourselves. We think we can have two Christmases and two currencies. We can build for ourselves mansions on earth and mansions in heaven and see one as a sign of the other – showing more about our goals than anything of heaven. We believe life is about our own mighty manors, building our very own little empires right here on earth.

We want God to role model after Santa. We want God to fulfill our dreams, the hopes we are working for, to grant our requests as we pray, or even better, like Santa, to make our dreams come true while we sleep with visions of sugarplums dancing through our heads.

We want God to fulfill our dreams, our hopes, and our expectations. However, Christ, The Tiger, didn't show up to teach us to pray in a way to make ourselves heard, to get God to work for us and to fulfill our dreams. A single reading through the gospels will clarify that God is both aware of our dreams and is rather unimpressed. If there is a judgment on our dreams, our desires, our passions, it's simply that we have the wrong ones.

Jesus doesn't just challenge our dreams, he encourages us to seek different ones, to get in touch with God's dreams, God's passions, God's goals for us and the world so that we could live them into reality. Jesus' way of praying was far different from just offering God our wish list. Jesus said, "When you pray, pray like this…"

> *Our Father in heaven,*
> *Hallowed be Your Name, (above all others),*
> *Your Kingdom Come, Your will be done,*
> *On earth as in heaven… (right here, right now)*

Jesus' prayer begins reminding us we are God's beloved. God is not some wrathful ruler, fearful deity, or divine punisher, but "Father." When you forget who and whose you are, then pray over and over, "Father…", "Father…", "Father…" This repetition will remind you that God loves you as you are, but also that God loves you too much to leave you that way, for your sake, and the world's. When we know we are beloved, then we can get busy living into God's dreams, God's wishes, God's kingdom. Contrary to popular approaches to prayer, Jesus didn't say, pray, "My kingdom come," but "Thy kingdom come," It's not God's job to align with our dreams for ourselves or the world but for us to align ourselves with God's dreams.

Now we come to the biggest challenge of all. Besides loving our two Christmases and our two currencies, most of all we love and put our trust in our two kingdoms.

Not long after the first Easter, the smart Emperors, Dictators, Rulers, including Presidents, over time have not fought Jesus on praying "Thy Kingdom Come." They pray right along, including "on earth as it is in heaven," but subtly they add these two words, "one day." The kingdom of God will come, one day, but until then Jesus is in heaven, seated at the right hand of the father, and until that future when God reigns supreme, we will just have to live with our two kingdoms.

One of the savviest applicators of the two kingdoms approach was Ivan Vasilyevich, also known as Ivan the Terrible, who ruled as Tsar of Russia. Notice the nice cross on his crown? For at least a thousand years, crosses came standard on every new crown. As a dictator, Ivan was so intense in his domination of Russia that it seemed he would never marry. At the suggestion of his advisors, Ivan sent aides on a search for a bride. They settled on Sophia, the daughter of the King of Greece.

Ivan asked the king for his daughter's hand. The King of Greece agreed as long as Ivan would convert to the Greek Orthodox Church. Ivan consented. As part of his profession of faith, he would be baptized along with five hundred of his soldiers. When Ivan learned more about Jesus' way in the world and the significance of baptism, he began to be concerned that he and his soldiers might not be able to go to war afterward. Apparently, Ivan the Terrible did not just join the church but read the book close enough to get a pretty clear sense of Jesus' way in the world. Ivan devised a solution. When he and five hundred of his army went into the water with five hundred priests for baptism by immersion, Ivan and his soldiers each extended their sword arms out of the water. They had joined the church with their bodies but left their swords and fighting arms unbaptized.

Clearly, he understood the two kingdoms, one in heaven, and one to do whatever 'needs to be' done on earth. We revel in our two Christmases, our two currencies, and of course our two kingdoms. We claim the freedom to choose neither over the other but blend the two no matter how absurd we become, as Kurt Vonnegut observed,

> *For some reason, the most vocal Christians among us never mention the Beatitudes (Matthew 5). But, often with tears in their eyes, they demand that the Ten Commandments be*

posted in public buildings. And of course, that's Moses, not Jesus. I haven't heard one of them demand that the Sermon on the Mount, the Beatitudes, be posted anywhere.

"Blessed are the merciful" in a courtroom? "Blessed are the peacemakers" in the Pentagon? Give me a break!"

We will continue to blend our two Christmases, our two currencies, and our two kingdoms, as long as God will allow. To our dismay, Jesus is no Santa. When he showed up on the shores of Galilee or anywhere else, it was not to be the fulfiller of our dreams, far from it. Instead, he worked diligently to wake us from our sleeping, from our Candy Land dreams, and call us into God's visions for the world.

Empires have risen, claimed the world, and lost it, only to try again under another flag. Even those claiming to be under God, or even the sole nation under God, all fall away, and, yet, again and again he comes. In the winter of the year, heralded by angels and surrounded by shepherds, or in the spring of the year to the frustration of soldiers and dismay of Empires, he comes, Christ the Tiger, loose in the world with God's dreams of what might be as we sing each year,

Joy to the world! The Lord has come
Let earth receive her King!
Let every heart prepare him room
And heaven and nature sing

Joy to the world! the Savior reigns
Let us our songs employ while fields and floods
Rocks, hills and plains repeat the sounding joy

He rules the world with truth and grace
And makes the nations prove
The glories of His righteousness
And wonders of His love.

The Controlling Crowd

Do you ever hear voices from your childhood? I do. I can still hear the promises. Like my parents, as they assured me, if I worked hard, then my hard work would pay off as I could create a life for myself and my future family.

I can still hear my teachers, encouraging me to study hard for every challenge, promising me if I would apply myself, get good grades, then I could go to any college I wanted and have whatever career I chose. I was eight. I did not know if I wanted to go to college. I didn't know if you needed to go to college to be an astronaut. They assured me that I did.

From my coaches, I still can hear their voices, calling me by my last name, "Jones! Hustle! Get in the game! Get in the game!" The promise was there, if I worked hard, I might get to become a 'starter'. I never made it. I was too slow. There wasn't a sport that by the time I got off the bench and into the game, half the season wasn't over. Still, I can hear them pushing me onward so that one day, I could drink from the cup of glory, whatever that was.

Among those voices, promising rewards for my effort, there was one other. A mysterious, legendary giant of a man. He promised me rewards for being good, tangible gifts of my own choosing to celebrate just how good I had been. He watched over me, paying close attention to who and how I was at home and at school, keeping track of everything I did, assuring me that if I was just good enough, I could make "The List". He got me so excited about what I might get that I could barely sleep trusting that I had been a good boy and would make the cut. I still remember what we said about him, what we sang about him.

He's making a list. He's checking it twice,
gonna find out who's naughty or nice...

He sees you when you're sleeping,
he knows when you're awake.
He knows when you've been bad or good,
so be good for goodness sake!

Besides being the mascot for *Macy's*, Santa gives the basic message of society, the one we were all raised to believe, and the one we'll likely pass on to our children, our cultural crowd's norm: *Do good, be good, and guaranteed, you'll be rewarded. Do poorly, be bad, and sooner or later, guaranteed, you'll be punished.* Too bad it's not Christian. It is corporate. It is karma. It is also Roman.

Rome used reward and punishment. Rome promised gain for those who "did well" and the threat of pain and punishment to those who failed to fall in line. The purpose of reward and punishment was to guide, shape, and if necessary, control the behaviour of people the leaders wanted to influence. The way of Rome can be classified as *External Control Psychology* which is a way of relating to people focusing on controlling others with motivators, rewards and punishment. William Glasser defined *External Control Psychology* as, *punish the people who are doing wrong, so they will do what we say is right; then reward them, so they keep doing what we want them to do.*

The Roman Way, or *Control Psychology*, is still the most common way nations relate to nations, nations relate to people, and people relate to each other. This approach of trying to control others through an effective motivator or stimulus, reward or punishment, or at least the promise of reward or threat of punishment, is the common practice in most areas of life. In commerce, marketers ask, "What benefit can we promise to entice consumers? What images or celebrities can we use to get others to buy our product or service?" In politics, "What can we say to get you to vote for our candidate?" In companies, "How can we get employees to increase productivity?" In churches, "How do we get people to come? How do we get people to participate? volunteer? give? believe?"

Many educators still commonly use reward and punishment in their attempts to guide students to set goals. Behaviorist B.F. Skinner said, "Give me a child, and I'll shape him into anything."

The Roman Way is still very popular among parents. Alphie Kohn in *Punished by Rewards* cites a list of parenting books with a reward and punish model of parenting: *Don't Be Afraid to Discipline; Parents in Charge – Parents in Control; Taking Charge; Back in Control; Disciplining Your Preschooler – and Feeling Good About It;* and, *'Cause I'm the Mommy, That's Why.*

The Roman Way has been adopted over time because it is often quite effective. It was in Rome. In an age of barbarians and civil war, into power rose Gaius Octavius, later named Augustus Caesar, one of the most effective and productive leaders in history. He defeated Julius Caesar's assassins and brought in an era known as the *Pax Romana,* or Roman Peace. He ruled Rome from twenty years before Jesus was born until Jesus was a youth. His accomplishments were many. He established peace and national unity after 100 years of civil war. He expanded Rome's Empire, law, and government. He established a sound economic policy and stable currency. He extended the highway system connecting Rome with its far-reaching empire. He built many channels and bridges. He fostered free trade among the provinces. He established an efficient postal service – the man even got the mail delivered on time!

To measure Jesus' effectiveness on a Roman Scale, Jesus doesn't move the meter. He doesn't even slightly tip the scale. He did nothing for his nation compared to what Augustus did for

Rome, but he never intended to. When given the opportunity to become the Jewish Caesar, Jesus refused, repeatedly.

Jesus rejected becoming the Jewish Caesar because promising a world of rewards for those who do well and threatening punishment for those who do poorly is dishonest. The real myth of Christmas is not Santa or the Magi, but the promise of guaranteed rewards for the good and punishment for the naughty. The world often rotates in exactly the opposite direction as it is often the unscrupulous who gain the largest rewards, those who use people as Rome did, as a means to an end to gain the goals they were trying to attain. In this system, those who do 'rightly' other than obey the present power, often go unrewarded, or worse.

In our history books, between the pages of one war after another, the maps of how one Empire conquered the land of another, there are a few stories which tell of individuals who did right exceptionally well but were far from rewarded, many were killed. What of their stories? Those who challenged the status quo of the way things are with a vision of grander possibilities, what usually happened to them?

The lesson of history, for those with eyes to see, if you do rightly, maybe you'll be rewarded, but if you are able to achieve the level of greatness in this world of truly doing right, you'll likely end up just like the other great ones before you - you may be poisoned in Athens, crucified in Jerusalem, or shot in Memphis.

Do well and be rewarded? Notice the cross in front of your worship space and remember what it meant to Jesus, what it represented to Jesus' followers before and after he died. The cross was the risk. The cross represented what might happen if you follow after Jesus, what might happen if you step out of the crowd, if you go against the flow of the status quo.

A minister was giving a tour of their newly renovated sanctuary to Clarence Jordan. Proudly, he pointed to the new center-piece of their worship space, a shiny cross that towered overhead. "It cost $10,000," the minister boasted, and was donated by one of our members."

Clarence just laughed his usual laugh and said, "There was a time when Christians could get them for free."

Gandhi also observed the disconnect between Jesus' life and teachings and our sanctuaries.

> "Stoning prophets and erecting churches to their memory afterwards has been the way of the world through the ages. Today we worship Christ, but the Christ in the flesh we crucified."

We turn our crosses into symbols of Jesus' victory and ignore them as symbols of possible consequences to following Jesus' call, living Jesus' way, and reminders of what might happen to all brave enough to step out in faith over fear. We overlook one of the biggest differences between Christianity and other large religions. Christianity is the only major religion whose central figure died horribly at a very young age. Buddha died around age eighty, surrounded by his followers. Confucius died an old man while he was putting together the ancient writings of the Chinese people. Muhammad died in the arms of his favourite wife while he was ruler of Arabia. Jesus died abandoned by his friends, nailed to a cross, seemingly betrayed by all including God, stripped of clothes, power, and dignity around age thirty-three.

Wasn't he good enough? Be good and you'll be rewarded? Do right and life will go well for you? Love others, and they'll love you and respect you? Jesus saw otherwise and prepared his followers. If they were going to step out for a different world as he did, then there was no reason to expect different treatment than what Jesus received. Jesus warned, Matthew 10,

> No disciple is above his or her teacher any more than a slave
> is above his or her master. If you are my disciple, then whatever

names I've been called, you may be called, and whatever happens to me may happen to you.

Jesus gave a similar warning, in Matthew 16,

If any of you want to become followers of mine, disciples of mine, then deny self, pick up your own cross, and follow me. If you're goal is to save your life, then you'll lose it, but if you let go of your life, in my way, you'll find it.

Jesus' Way was not do right and be rewarded but do right regardless. Jesus' Way was not do well and benefit but do well regardless. Jesus' Way was not love to be loved but love regardless. Jesus' Way was simply do right, do well, and love – regardless.

William Glasser defines the opposite of *Control Psychology* as *Choice Psychology*. That is Jesus' Way – we can always choose. As Viktor Frankl discovered in the concentration camps during World War II,

Everything can be taken from a man but one thing: the last of the human freedoms—to choose one's attitude in any given set of circumstances, to choose one's own way.

The Roman Way was promising reward or threatening punishment and convincing their subjects they ultimately had no other choice than to comply. The Roman Way was symbolized in the coin and the cross, though today we use simpler, softer, symbols, the carrot and the stick. Both symbolize a dehumanizing of persons into beasts or commodities to be controlled, or worse, bought and sold. Jesus did not try to control others. Instead, he taught people to claim their humanity by claiming their freedom to choose their response in every situation, which is why Rome ultimately kept trying to stop the Christian Movement. For an Empire based on control, nothing aggravates them more than people who understand they can always choose regardless of what others do or what happens. Robin Meyers relates,

> In an Empire crawling with gods, Rome allowed all sorts of local religious beliefs and practices to flourish, as long as loyal subjects of the realm also worshiped Caesar. Whether it was the Mithraism of Persia, with its ritual slaughter of bulls, or the Egyptian cults of Isis and Osiris, competing religions surrounded the early Christians—just as they do today. What is vitally important to remember, however, is that when these first Jesus People encountered such rival faiths, they responded in a strange and unexpected way. They did not fashion creeds and demand that they be taken as vows. Rather they simply refused to worship Caesar, stopped practicing animal sacrifice, threw open the doors of their underground assemblies to all who would come, redistributed wealth, and made the dangerous claim that "Jesus Christ was Lord." They would pray for the emperor, but not to him.

In 203, five Christians were sentenced to death for being Christians. One was named Vibia Perpetua. She was twenty-two, a mother of a young boy. Her father begged her to renounce her faith, but she refused. "See that pot over there, father? If we were to call it by another name, wouldn't it still be a pot? No more can I be called something other than Christian."

Jesus' Way was her way. Even a 'powerless' twenty-two year old woman as a Christ-like one could stand in front of Rome no matter what the threat. In an age where this word's meaning is almost lost, she modeled the Latin *integritas,* our integrity. She was other than a beast to be controlled with threat or potential reward, she was a person. She could choose. No one, not even Rome could remove her integrity. She was a Tiger among tigers who had given up their stripes to become goats, prodded with a stick or led by a carrot.

Jesus didn't reject becoming a Jewish Caesar or a World Caesar because he didn't think he could achieve it, he just rejected the Roman Way for a better way. He rejected trying to control others or even the world through dehumanizing reward and punishment. Jesus lifted up the power of choice and the value of persons. And Jesus lifted up the most human and the most powerful choice above all, love.

In the arena, Perpetura was attacked by a wild boar and then stabbed with a sword. Before her death, she encouraged others to, "Stand fast in the faith and love one another." The Way was clear. Claim your power to choose, and choose love.

The Commanding Crowd

In Matthew 22, a lawyer comes to test Jesus and asks, "Which one of the commandments is the greatest?"

> Jesus replied, "The greatest commandment is, 'You shall love the Lord your God with all your heart, and with all your soul, and with all your mind.' And the second greatest commandment is, 'You shall love your neighbor as yourself.'"

The Roman rule was enforced by the most powerful Empire in the world with the greatest military force and the ultimate in capital punishment, the cross. Caligula, one of the cruelest of all the Roman rulers, said,

> Crosses and corpses are so educational. Let the scum see their blood or the blood of some of their kin and it will so cower them in fear that then we can rule them.

The Romans were masters at intimidation and threat. Such a power could order much, command much, and demand much, except for one central thing no empire or authority can command with any effect, love. Command all you want, demand all you wish, no power in the world can force love.

When the lawyer asks Jesus, "What's the greatest commandment?" he is asking a question of authority. He wants to know where Jesus assigned power. For example, if Jesus said, "Obey God," then God has the power. If he said, "Obey the laws of the scripture," then the law and those who interpret it have the power. If he says, "Be loyal to Rome," then Rome has the power. Rules require rulers. Commandments require commanders. Even laws require lawyers to interpret them and police to enforce them. The power is in the lawmakers, the order keepers, the rulers who make and interpret the rules.

Rome sought control through reward and punishment, but what use are rewards and punishments in love? They have no power or authority as love comes from the choice of the lover. If someone chooses not to love, what can you do? Nothing will work. The power is in the one loving or choosing not to love. Not only can love not be commanded, but love cannot be stopped. You cannot stop someone from loving if they have chosen, committed, and devoted their lives to loving. Jesus shifts the power from the empires to the lovers.

Jesus walks into the world of Empires and Emperors, into the large National Empire of Rome, the Religious Empire of Jerusalem, and the patriarchal family empires, and with an answer dethrones all the rulers from their thrones of domination, setting the captives free. Jesus liberated his followers to choose, and to make the greatest choice – love, as William Sloane Coffin pointed out,

> Love (is Jesus') answer to legalism on the one hand and lawlessness on the other. Love hallows individuality. Love consecrates and never desecrates personality. Love demands that all our actions reflect a movement toward and not away from nor against each other. And love insists that all people assume their responsibility for all their relations.

For Rome, the cross was the powerful hammer to stop any threat, but in Jesus, the cross lost its efficacy. Instead of the ultimate threat, it became a symbol for a love that couldn't be stopped. Jesus chose love, regardless. At his arrest, Jesus called Judas, "Friend." Was Jesus ignorant to what "friends" were supposed to be? No. He just would not let Judas decide how he was going to be toward him or in the world. History would call Judas, "The Betrayer," the "Traitor," and even, "The one with a devil." Jesus called him, "Friend." Why? Because Jesus didn't give up his power to choose love.

On the cross Jesus prayed, "Father forgive them because they don't know what they are doing." While suffering the most painful and humiliating suffering Rome could imagine, he still chose forgiveness – not because he had to – but because he could. Forgiveness was and is a choice, not because we are virtuous, or especially saintly, but for Christ-like ones, we know power when we see it. Forgiving is power, turning the other cheek, giving your shirt if someone steals your coat, going the second mile, all are powers no one can take away.

Willard Waller, who ironically was born in Walla Walla, Washington, was a sociologist who wrote about *The Principle of Least Interest*. Waller's central thesis is, "In any relationship, there is an inverse relationship between love and power. Whoever loves the most has the least power, and whoever loves least has the most power." For example, if in a marriage, you love someone tremendously who doesn't care about you, the carefree one has the most power according to Waller.

Jesus would disagree. For Jesus, whoever loves most has the most power because they choose how they want to be in the world. The difference is that for Waller, love is dependence on the person or object you love in the belief that if your love is returned then all will be well. Jesus speaks of love as a freeing force. The only way love loses its power is if love is used to try and control others. "See how much I love you? Look what you're doing to me." The cross was not a passive aggressive attempt to punish others by Jesus' own suffering, to guilt or shame the world into change. Love is a greater power as long as it neither controls nor is controlled but involves choice.

If love is your way, you love not in hopes of gaining, influencing, or even controlling others or the world around you. You love because you can.

Closer than Waller to Jesus' understanding of love was Pierre Teilhard de Chardin who wrote,

Someday, after mastering the winds, the waves, the tides and gravity, we shall harness for God the energies of love, and then, for a second time in the history of the world, man will have discovered fire.

The Lower the Bar Crowd

In the movie, *City Slickers*, Billy Crystal plays Mitch, a New York City Salesman, father, and husband, who is facing his upcoming 39th birthday with the joy of a wake.

In order to spark some life back in him, his friends give him a two-week vacation out west to a dude ranch in Colorado to participate in a cattle drive.

On the drive, Mitch is moving part of the herd with Curly, a full-fledged real life rugged cowboy.

> Curly asks, "How old are you? Thirty-eight?"
>
> "Thirty-nine," Mitch replies.
>
> "You all come up here about the same time with the same problems. You spend fifty weeks out of the year getting knots in your rope and think two weeks up here will get them out. None of you see it. You know the secret of life?"
>
> "No," Mitch replies, "what."
>
> "This." Curly holds up one finger.
>
> "Your finger?" Mitch asks.
>
> "One thing. Just one thing. You stick to that and everything else (falls in place)?"
>
> "What's that one thing?" Mitch asks.
>
> "That's what you've got to figure out."

So, what is Jesus' One Thing? What set Jesus apart from all other leaders religious and otherwise in the world? What did Jesus expect from his followers that is distinctly Jesus and therefore distinctly Christian? Love. Perhaps no where is this clearer than when Jesus declares his "One Thing" compared to how others saw it over time.

Most religions have a "Golden Rule," or a "One Thing," but Jesus' version is significantly different. See if you notice the difference. I listed Jesus' version first.

Do to others as you would have them do to you.
Luke 6:31

Do not do to others what you would not like yourself.
Then there will be no resentment against you,
either in the family or in the state.
Confucius, Analects 12:2

Hurt not others in ways that you yourself
would find hurtful.
Buddha, Udana-Varga 5,1

This is the sum of duty; do naught onto others what you would
not have them do unto you.
Hinduism, Mahabharata 5,1517

The definitive difference is that the other "Golden Rules" are cited in the negative. "<u>Do not do</u> to others what you <u>do not</u> want done to you." Jesus' version is in the affirmative. It is not lived out by not doing toward others what you don't want, but by doing toward others what you do want.

Imagine a debate on love between Islam and Christianity. In this imaginary debate, we've brought back two of the most charismatic speakers in American history. Representing Islam is Malcolm X. Representing Christianity is Martin Luther King, Jr. Malcolm X speaks first,

I believe in the brotherhood of man, all men, but I don't believe in brotherhood with anybody who doesn't want brotherhood with me. I believe in treating people right, but I'm not going to waste my time trying to treat somebody right who doesn't know how to return the treatment...

You and I have to preserve the right to do what is necessary to bring an end to (injustice), and it doesn't mean that I advocate violence, but at the same time I am not against using violence in self-defense. I don't even call it violence when it's self-defense, I call it intelligence.

Malcolm finishes his remarks with poignant, passionate, and memorable phrases.

Concerning non-violence: it is criminal to teach a man not to defend himself when he is the constant victim of brutal attacks...

I don't advocate violence; but if a man steps on my toes, I'll step on his...

Sometimes you have to pick the gun up to put the Gun down...

Martin Luther King takes the podium and starts out slowly.

Jesus says, "Love your enemies," (because) love has within it a redemptive power. And there is a power there that eventually transforms individuals... Just keep loving them, and they can't stand it too long. Oh, they react in many ways in the beginning. They react with guilt feelings, and sometimes they'll hate you a little more at that transition period, but just keep loving them. And by the power of your love they will break down

under the load. That's love, you see. It is redemptive, and this is why Jesus says love. There's something about love that builds up and is creative. There is something about hate that tears down and is destructive. So love your enemies.

Then, like a train, he picks up momentum, focusing now on the ineffectiveness of violence,

Violence never really deals with the basic evil of the situation. Violence may murder the murderer, but it doesn't murder murder. Violence may murder the liar, but it doesn't murder lie; it doesn't establish truth. Violence may even murder the dishonest man, but it doesn't murder dishonesty. Violence may go to the point of murdering the hater, but it doesn't murder hate. It may increase hate. It is always a descending spiral leading nowhere. This is the ultimate weakness of violence: It multiplies evil and violence in the universe. It doesn't solve any problems.

Having heard the two men in this imaginary debate, who would you say won? Who would you say represents your views? Who would you say has the philosophy you want to see in the next election of your political leaders?

The difference in the teaching of Jesus and all other religious leaders is the height of the bar Jesus set for his followers in regard to love which including not only "don't do what you don't want done to you," but the proactive "do unto others what you'd want done to you and for you." Jesus level of love includes not just allies but enemies. It is Jesus' Way as clearly stated in Matthew 5,

You have heard the standard, "Love your neighbour and hate your enemy," but I say, "Love your enemies, pray for those who seek to hurt you. Those are children who behave like God is their Father. God causes his sun to shine on both evil and good, and sends rain to the

righteous and unrighteous. So let your love be without condition. If you love those who love you, how does that show growth? Even the most unscrupulous can love like that. If you only greet brothers and sisters, are you doing more than any others?

Christians often end prayers, "In Jesus' name." It has been so overly used it has lost its meaning. Even though "in Jesus' name" is often used as a divine formula for God's blessing, the phrase points less to the power of the name spoken but instead the identity and responsibility of those who claim the name. In Jesus' day, if you took on the name of someone, it meant you were part of their group, their family. To pray, "in Jesus name" meant a promise to not only try and pray as Jesus prayed but live as Jesus lived, like any disciple would for his teacher. To pray, "in Jesus name" is a pledge to "live continually in Jesus' way."

When Jesus' followers wanted to seek greatness, he challenged them to be the greatest in love. Let's make that our competition. Everyone gives their religion the blue ribbon, everyone rewards their faith with the gold medal, let's compete in love. If Jesus doesn't set the bar highest in love, then all other ways are taken. We can compete with the greatest architecture of our time in Jesus' name with buildings to last for 'eternity', but that was the way of the Egyptians. We can compete in 'truth' in Jesus' name, but that was the way of the Greeks. We can compete as the most moral people following our laws to the letter, but that was the way of the Jews. We can compete in the largest Empire in Jesus' name, but that was the way of the Romans. We can compete for inner peace and enlightenment in Jesus' name, but that's the way of the Buddhists. All that's left is love. Everything else that came before Jesus has been tried while the world remains relatively unchanged. We still live the Egyptian Way of seeking immortality through buildings and institutions. We still live the Greek Way of trying to answer every problem. We still live the Jewish Way of trying to solve every problem with a policy or procedure. We still live the Roman Way of control through promise of reward and threat of punishment. Unless Jesus advanced love as something other than glorified pacifism but as a way to change the world, then he is redundant.

Rabbi Harold Kushner, author of When Bad Things Happen to Good People, was asked why Jews don't believe that Jesus is the Messiah. He replied,

> *The reason Jews don't believe Jesus is the Christ is because when we look at the world, we don't see the messianic reign the prophets foretold. There is still war, the oppressed are still oppressed, the prisoners are not set free, the poor still suffer in poverty. We don't believe Jesus is the Messiah because to us the world seems just the same to us as before Jesus was born.*

Perhaps the time of confession of the church has come, not to our sins, but our refusal to live in Jesus' name, to live out Jesus' Way. We've been much too content to blend into or historical or contemporary crowds. We'll spend with the consumers at Christmas, vote with the kingdom crowd in November, and complain about immortality from our pulpits without requiring maturity from the pews, we'll limit our faith into a way of thinking so that much can be spoken while little actually changes. We will give up our freedom to act, freedom to love, and overuse our freedom of speech. Let us acknowledge the difference between Jesus' Way and our way, let us confess what author G.K. Chesterton said years ago,

> *Christianity has not been tried and found wanting; it has been found difficult and not tried.*

The Bullying Crowd

What crowd is this?

It's what the world would be like if we lived by the "eye for an eye, and tooth for a tooth" rule. Here's what Jesus had to say, Matthew 5,

> *You have heard the saying, "An eye for an eye, and a tooth for a tooth. I say to you, instead, do not resist a doer of evil. If anyone strikes you on your right cheek, turn to them your other cheek. If anyone wants to sue you and take your outer garment, give them your underwear. If anyone forces you to carry a pack for a mile, go a second mile.*

These three "If anyone..." statements Jesus offers here are less commandments of "Thou must" and more illustrations of what Jesus' way of love looks like. To understand Jesus' Way of love it's helpful to look at these illustrations in their original context and how parents can teach children how to live it out, or in our case, how our child has taught us.

Carrie and I disagree on how to prepare our children for life in the world where they are far from our overly protective gaze and reach. When we get them alone, away from each other, we have taught them our own perspectives on life, especially where violence is concerned. Carrie's response to a tyrant is this. "If someone is threatening you or bullying you, just walk away, and if you have to, run away." That is a nice approach, but I tell them different. "If you are threatened by a bully, and they back you into a corner, then hit them twice, two shots, pop-pop, right to the nose." I figure two shots is a good call in case they miss on the first. What I have found is that most bullies are lazy. They are looking for power the easy way. If you cause them trouble, and pain, they will leave you alone. Of course, you may be in an all in all brawl, but even then, at least you are up two hits to none. Given these two approaches to violence, Nathan considered them both and chose neither.

One Friday night, we were at the local high school football game. Cayla, our oldest, was with the band. Abbie and Nathan were playing with the mass of kids in the grass beyond the end zone. Nathan, then ten years old, came back to check in and made the comment, "It's weird over there."

"What do you mean?" I asked.

"Weird," he said. That's all.

He went back. After a while, I thought I'd go check on him and see just how weird it might be in the land beyond the boundary lines of the football field. As I walked up to the area, I saw 100 kids, 8 to 13, running around in packs with no adult in sight. "Lord of the Flies," I thought to myself. Then I saw Nate. Between us was a pack of boys with one out front, taunting Nate, pointing at him, throwing some paper at him supported and encouraged by those behind him.

"They are picking on my son," I realized.

I walked faster, intently looking around the boys and to Nate's face. His eyes were wide, but not from fear, I could see no anxiety on his face. His eyes were wide, and he was smiling.

I put my hand on the boy's shoulder that was taunting my child and said, "That's my son. Let's give him some space."

"Okay," he said, after all, to a ten year old, I'm huge. I then moved my hand from the boy to Nathan and put myself between him and the group. "Time to go," I said. We walked off together. I wondered how he was feeling. I looked for signs of fear, anxiety, or relief. I asked, "You okay?"

What I heard I did not expect, laughter, giggling. "Yeah," he said. "I'm okay." I did not know how to interpret Nathan's mood or his actions. He did not punch the boy or run away. He stood, looked him in the face, and smiled.

Three days later, I asked him, "Nate, when those boys at the football game were picking at you, what were you thinking?"

He responded, "They were humiliating." What he meant was, "They were humiliating themselves." They had attempted to intimidate him, frighten him, and shame him, but he would have none of it.

My son not only understands the Sermon on the Mount better than I do but apparently is a Zen master as well. One teacher advised, "An insult is like a gift, if you choose not to receive it, then it must go back to the giver." With the circle of boys surrounding him, Nate refused their attempt to humiliate him, and in his words, "They were humiliating themselves."

The three illustrations Jesus gives of turning the other cheek, giving your underwear, and carrying a pack the extra mile are all examples of how someone might stay beloved in an attempt from others to dominate or shame them into a lower status or caste than Beloved, Child of God.

When Jesus first cites the ancient code, "An eye for an eye and a tooth for a tooth," he is not citing an antiquated ethic but a morality that was a limitation on violent revenge and payback for wrongs incurred. "An eye for an eye" legislates a proportionate response. If someone pokes out someone's eye, then you or the broader community can poke out their eye in response in the name of justice. However, if someone pokes out your eye, you can't kill them. Killing them would be a disproportionate response. Illustrating the way of love, Jesus advances proportionate response to gracious response which allows the lover to see themselves and the offender as beloved of God.

If anyone strikes you on the right cheek, turn the other also. The detail in Jesus' scenario shows this isn't a bar room brawl or a fist fight in anger. The key is, "If anyone strikes you on the *right* cheek." Have you ever wondered why the right cheek? A blow by the right fist or a right slap would land on the left cheek. To hit the right cheek with a fist would require using the left hand but there are two givens: 1) most people are right handed and would strike right hand to left cheek 2) in Jesus' world, the left hand was used only for unclean tasks, like bathroom duties, and not for touching others. The only way for someone to strike the right cheek is not with a fist or openhanded slap but with the back of the hand. This is not a fight. This is an insult. The intention here is not to injure but to humiliate. To strike a social equal with a fist was a penalty of a day's wage. To strike an equal with a back of the hand insult was 100 days wages. A backhand slap to a lesser servant, female, or a child was usually the way of dealing with inferiors for which there was no penalty.

Turning the other cheek robs the person of the power to insult. They can no longer strike you in a back handed shaming fashion, they can only hit you right hand to left cheek, which, in their action, would declare publicly that you are their equal. Turning the cheek neither takes Carrie's advice to run away or my advice to swing for their nose. Instead, Jesus' Way stays present and challenges the person who would humiliate you to choose otherwise. Regardless, by neither accepting the humiliation or responding in violence, the person struck doesn't give up his or her ability to respond in the situation and the one who would humiliate ends up humiliated.

What Nathan exhibited at the football game and what Jesus calls for here are not the ways of fear, but courage. Read how Gandhi spoke of this nonviolent approach to people who threaten you.

Non-violence is not a cover for cowardice, but it is the supreme virtue of the brave. Exercise of non-violence requires far greater bravery than that of swordsmanship. Cowardice is wholly inconsistent with non-  *violence. Translation from swordsmanship to non-violence is possible and, at times, even an easy stage. Non-violence, therefore, presupposes ability to strike. It is a conscious deliberate restraint put upon one's desire for vengeance. But vengeance is any day superior to passive, effeminate and helpless submission. Forgiveness is higher still. Vengeance too is weakness. The desire for vengeance comes out of fear of harm, imaginary or real. A dog barks and bites when he fears. A man who fears no one on earth would consider it too troublesome even to summon up anger against one who is vainly trying to injure him. The sun does not wreak vengeance upon little children who throw dust at him. They only harm themselves in the act.*

If anyone wants to sue you and take your coat, give your cloak as well. This is a case for someone who has sunk deeper and deeper into poverty. Picture the courtroom. The poor person with no ability to pay his or her debts is forced by court and creditor to give the last thing he or she owns – his or her clothes. A clearer translation of Jesus' words is, "If anyone wants to sue you and take your outer garment, give them your undergarment as well." After giving his cloak, the poor man is standing there in front of everyone in his underwear, shamed by his creditor who holds his clothes and the court who forced him to give them over, made an example for all to see the shame in not paying what you owe. If the man then follows Jesus' advice and seemingly advances the humiliation, he takes off his underwear and gives it to his creditor.

While it might seem quite shameful and that the poor man just humiliated himself, in Jesus culture, being naked was taboo, and shame fell more on the person who would cause someone to be naked in public than on the naked person. By stripping, the debtor has taken shame from himself and given it to the creditor. The creditor is revealed not to be a legitimate moneylender but a punitive person at heart leaving someone in such a chilly state. More than likely the creditor would give back not only the underclothes but the cloak as well.

My friend Etta Britt's mother gave her a creative way to fight a pack of bullies without running away or hitting them in their noses. Here is her story,

> We had PE, physical education classes back then as well. We had to "dress out" everyday. It was a lovely outfit. Blue shorts, a gray t-shirt, tall athletic socks and tennis shoes. I enjoyed it though. We got to climb ropes, jump on trampolines, walk on the balance beams and do calisthenics. After class, all the girls would go to our locker room to change. Everyday I would start playing the school's fight song on the lockers as if they were a set of drums. The girls always joined in and we'd sing at the top of our lungs. There was one group of girls that didn't care for me though. Maybe it was because I loved to sing and dance and laugh a lot.
>
> One day I got wind they were plotting to embarrass me. They planned to wait until I was fully dressed, grab me and throw me into the shower. I was very upset about the news and went home and told my mother. The next morning, Mama handed me a bag. She said, "Melissa, here's what I want you to do. I have put a change of clothes in this bag. After class, put the clothes you are wearing now back on. When you see the girls coming toward you, run into the shower room, stand under the shower and turn it on yourself". I couldn't believed my mother

98

was actually telling me to get into the shower with my clothes on so I asked her why she wanted me to do this. She told me that if I did it myself, the girls would be powerless and would then leave me alone.

After class, I went to the locker room and got dressed. I played the fight song on the lockers as usual and carried on my business acting as if nothing was going on. I looked up and saw them coming. Four girls with evil in their eyes. I turned around and started walking toward the shower room. As the pace picked up behind me, I sprinted into the room and jumped under one of the shower heads. I turned on the water and let it drip down my head and onto my clothes. I then looked at the girls with a big smile and waved at them. They were stopped in their tracks and stunned. Just like my mother said, they were powerless. They turned around and left. I got out, got dressed in my fresh clothes, brushed my hair and left the locker room never to be bothered by them again.

Another brilliant idea from my mother.

If anyone forces you to go one mile, go also the second mile. Israel was an occupied territory. Roman soldiers could force someone to carry their pack, but in order to limit what the soldiers could do, a soldier could only force a person to go one mile. Then they could find another person for the next mile. The conscription showed the power difference between soldier and occupied citizen.  All such duties reminded the occupied country of their less than Roman status. A Jew living by Jesus' Way responds to the soldier's command to carry his pack with, "Sure." The soldier is surprised at the seeming joy for the task and the noticeable lack of resentment. According to the law, after a mile, the soldier asks for his pack back. If he volunteers to go the second mile, a forced duty has now become a choice, what was required has now become a gift. In a more comical result, the Jew might say, "No," to the request to return the pack and start walking faster down the road. The once commanding soldier has become the chaser asking for his pack back because he knows that if he forces someone to go beyond the one mile limit, he would be in trouble. The people of Israel were used to seeing one of their own forced by a Roman to carry his pack. They were not used to seeing a Roman chasing a Jew asking for his pack back. By carrying the pack an extra mile, the one in Jesus' Way refuses humiliation and walks with honor. He also gives the soldier a chance to see the 'second rate citizen of an oppressed land' as a first rate person.

As a rule to obey, 'Turn the other cheek,'" won't go far. As a creative example of love lived, it opens an infinite array of choices for many situations across cultures and time. That high level of love enacted requires not just love but hope and faith as Gandhi observed,

> Nonviolence is impossible without a living faith in God. A non-violent person can do nothing save by the power and grace of God. Without it he won't have the courage to die without anger, without fear and without retaliation. Such courage comes from the belief that God sits in the hearts of all and that there should be no fear in the presence of God. The knowledge of the omnipresence of God also means respect for the lives even of those who may be called opponents.

The Jesus Crowd

Jesus did not have an administrative assistant to set his schedule. We don't have old copies of Jesus' calendar so that we can see the persons and groups Jesus intended to meet. His encounters often seem random, as if there was no plan, and the people Jesus met were haphazard – like the woman who happens to be at the well in the middle of the day or the blind beggar on the outskirts of Jericho. However, perhaps Jesus wasn't just going away from crowds but instead headed toward particular individuals. If Jesus had a calendar, it might have listed the names of these individuals, one by one. For Jesus, they would have been more than appointments and agenda items, but each a person a distinct encounter, like this woman. While others had to stand up to family, religious crowds, even soldiers to claim their place in the world as beloved of God, she had a unique challenge. She had to stand up to Jesus. Here is their encounter in Mark 7,

Jesus journeyed with the disciples to the region of Tyre. Upon arrival, Jesus secretly entered a house.

A woman whose little daughter had an unclean spirit immediately heard about him, and she came and bowed down at his feet. The woman was not Jewish but a Gentile of Syrophoenician origin. She begged Jesus to help her daughter.

Jesus replied, "Let the children be fed first, for it is not fair to take the children's food and throw it to dogs."

She answered Jesus, "But sir, even the dogs under the table get to eat the children's crumbs."

Jesus laughed and affirmed her answer. He said, "You may go, the demon has left your daughter. She is well."

The woman went home and found her daughter lying on the bed, the demon gone.

The next day, Jesus and the disciples left the area.

Imagine you are this woman. You have heard that Jesus was coming. Your daughter is ill, and you have been unable to help her, so you go looking for Jesus. The rumors you heard about him are enough to make you cross whatever social barriers there are to see if he can heal your child. Even those closest to you daunt you, "He won't see you," or "They won't let you in." Their discouragement might have been enough to stop you, but you weren't just going for yourself.

You get through your friends and Jesus' followers, and you see him, your hope. You take the position of subservience; you fall to his feet as a beggar seeking mercy from the only one you believe can help you. Pleading, you cry out, "My daughter is ill. Can you... Will you please help her?"

Jesus does not raise you up. He does not lift you from the floor. He speaks down to you in a condescending attitude as if the floor is where you belong. Why does he not lift you up as the rumors say he had lifted others? He speaks to you as you were afraid he might, rejecting you and your request, rejecting your daughter. He confirms your fear with an insult, "Let the children be fed first, for it is not fair to take the children's food and throw it to the dogs."

Essentially, Jesus says, "I'm here for the children of Israel, the children of God, not your child, and not you or your daughter. There is not enough to go around – not enough food, not enough love, not enough help. No one throws scarce food meant for the children to dogs – like you. Now, go away." Jesus insults you, your gender, your race, and your people. Jesus tells you that you are less than a person and so is your daughter, you are less than human, you are dogs and don't deserve help.

Jesus, who had earlier, taught, "Don't let evil things come out of you," lets the insults fly, and does so at the dinner table, not only an important symbol in Judaism, but for the early church, and for Jesus. While he had given many sinners, traitors, and social reprobates places at the table, here he denies this woman her very right to health and life for her child and gives her a metaphor that not only doesn't allow her a seat at the table – Jesus puts her under it.

Most of us have difficulty imagining Jesus being rude. There are multiple excuses granted to Jesus in commentaries for this behavior, "He was tired and hungry. This just shows he's human, we can all be rude when we are tired and hungry." "Because Jesus was human, he had his own bigotries and prejudices." "If you knew the Syrophoenicians and the evil they had done over time, you'd see she deserved it." Even with these excuses, the Gospel writer would likely have not included it unless Jesus was intentionally rude for a purpose.

These excuses overlook the underlying implication of Jesus' journey. Though this woman is an intruder to their dinner, it may be that she's the very reason that Jesus came. The encounter begins in Mark with, "Jesus left from there and went away to the region of Tyre," and after the encounter, the next day, "Then he returned from the region of Tyre." Jesus travels, encounters her, and the next day returns. Perhaps she was the only reason for the journey. There are no other encounters. While in this region, Jesus didn't go see any of the Jews living there, didn't go meet with any leaders or philosophers, didn't go to any place of teaching or worship, didn't meet with any government leaders. Though she seems like an intruder, she may have been exactly the person he traveled to see, the encounter he expected, the moment he wanted. If so, then perhaps this insult is just the gift she needed from him for her to claim her place as a beloved daughter of God.

Jesus challenged her with the insult, but he also gave her other images: children of God, a table, and the house of God. Though Jesus threw scarcity at her, he offered her images of abundance in God's house. Because it is God's house, the rules change, and she knows it. If God does love humanity, and God does love her, then it is a Godly love. It doesn't rank on value but gives value. There is nothing she can do to make God love her more, but because she is loved, there is a lot she can do – even challenge Jesus if he limits God's love.

When she comes, she goes to the floor. That's the appropriate social place for a Syrophonecian woman coming uninvited, without permission to the presence of a Jewish man. He affirms her self-placement, "You are lower, down there with the dogs." To be beloved of God, we must claim it. Jesus lets her. Here is how she does it. First, she doesn't argue the insult, but accepts it as a gift. Even a dog in the house of God is loved with God's infinite love. You cannot add to an infinite love. So in the Master's house, in the house of an infinite value giving love of God, even the dogs are loved infinitely. If the children are loved more, infinity plus one, it is still infinity. She does not debate Jesus' insult; she removes it of all power by placing herself at the table of God, the God of infinite love. Granted, she may not have known the math or added infinity plus one, but she felt it. At God's table, it does not matter if you come as Moses or a mutt, sit at it or beneath it. The table is God's table and therefore a wondrous place to be.

Jesus also gives her another hint. Bread. He implied that there is not enough bread for her or her family and that God's chosen get it first. The crowd says, "My group not yours," or, much more subtly, the crowd says, "My group – then yours, later." The crowd accepts an idea of justice for the whole world, an image where no one will hunger – one day. Jesus says, "Let the children be fed first," not that you won't get food, medicine, love, "That will come one day, just be patient."

In Turkey, there is a longstanding tradition of when a woman sees a bird near her house or land on a windowsill, she says, "Haberes Buenos." Haberes means 'news' and Buenos means 'good.' The hope is the bird will bring good news about why women are always placed in a subservient role to men.

The tradition is rooted in legend. Long ago, women asked King Solomon why men were allowed to marry more than one woman but women weren't allowed the same right. Even wise King Solomon was stumped. He replied, "Only God knows." Well the women weren't satisfied with that answer, so Solomon said, "Let's ask God." Solomon wrote the question on a piece of parchment and tied it to the leg of a bird. Solomon sent the bird to flight with the instruction of taking the message to God and not to come back without an answer.

So, the women keep waiting, they look to birds and ask, "Good news?" But the birds come empty handed. So, they wait, accepting the world as is, hoping that God, King, men, or some government or organization will value them and raise them from their position of less-than to a place of equality, of mutual status as valued and beloved.

Injustice is promoted as "the will of God" as others since have sited the place of women, slaves, other nations, all part of God's hierarchy for the blessing and benefit of those in power. There is another answer, not that injustice is the will of God, but that one day, like the slaves in Egypt, God will make a way. For now, the faithful are to wait. Jesus uses both with the woman, her place at the floor is just, and she will have to wait for the children of Israel to be fed first as there is not enough bread for everyone.

Again, she is onto him. This of course is Jesus, the guy who feeds five thousand people with five loaves and two fish. Here, Jesus speaks of scarcity, "There is not enough food to go around, but maybe one day." Hidden in the image of bread, she gets the wink. Jesus' metaphor points again to abundance. There is room, now. There is plenty, here. She answers him, "Sir, even the dogs under the table eat the children's crumbs."

She speaks of a limitless power of God where even the crumbs, the leftovers, the discarded is more than enough. So, she refused to accept insult because she believed that God was abundantly loving  and gracious. She claimed her place. She would not be forced to take an assigned space in a world where some are the beloved of God and some are dogs. She would not accept an image of God that valued one race, one people, one gender higher than another, one at the table and one below it. She claimed a value giving love, and for her, the categories of the crowd disappeared. For her to wait and not claim her place at the table would have been a sign of a terrible lack of faith.

Jesus affirmed her answer. In my imagination, though not in the text, he laughed and smiled at her, affirming her bold stance, affirming her refusal to wait on God, government, Jesus, or any other to claim her place as beloved child of God, at God's table, and God's kingdom. Then Jesus sent her on her way telling her that her daughter is well.

The next day, Jesus left the area. Perhaps she is why he came, but not for her alone. Perhaps it was for so much more. By challenging her to take her place as beloved at the table of God, Jesus encouraged her to take a stand, and she became a model for the rest of the area. She overcame what Henri Nouwen refers to as our greatest temptation,

Over the years, I have come to realize that the greatest trap in our life is not success, popularity, or power, but self-rejection. Success, popularity, and power can indeed present a great temptation, but their seductive quality often comes from the

way they are part of the much larger temptation of self-rejection. When we have come to believe in the voices that call us worthless and unlovable, then success, popularity, and power are easily perceived as attractive solutions. The real trap, however, is self-rejection. As soon as someone accuses me or criticizes me, as soon as I am rejected, left alone, or abandoned, I find myself thinking, "Well, that proves once again that I am a nobody." ... [My dark side says,] I am no good... I deserve to be pushed aside, forgotten, rejected, and abandoned. Self-rejection is the greatest enemy of the spiritual life because it contradicts the sacred voice that calls us the "Beloved." Being the Beloved constitutes the core truth of our existence."

Because she stood up to Jesus and claimed for herself her place as beloved, she could encourage others to do the same. Perhaps this text was in the gospel because of her, she was remembered throughout the area as the woman who would not wait and who would not take less than "Beloved," for an answer, not even from Jesus, and she encouraged others to do the same.

While we often place power in the Empires, it is the power of single individuals taking a stand that begin true social change, as Scott Peck observed,

> *The whole course of human history may depend on a change of heart in one solitary and even humble individual.... For it is in the solitary mind and soul of the individual that the battle between good and evil is waged and ultimately won or lost.*

She may have set a fire that transformed all of Tyre, not just for herself, but for her daughter, and for all the generations to come.

The Wait Crowd

The Syrophonecian woman didn't wait on government, God, or even God's Messiah to claim her place as beloved of God. She didn't have to prove she was worthy. Her worth came from value given to her in the love of God. Not even Jesus or Jesus' spokesperson could take that from her, which is exactly the out of the crowd behavior Jesus has always sought, the type of courageous action that could claim a seat at the table of God or on a public bus.

When Rosa Parks wanted to ride the public bus, in Montgomery, Alabama, in the 1940's, she had to enter the front door, pay the fare, exit, and then reboard through the bus's back door. In 1943, a tired Rosa Parks entered the bus, did not exit to reenter, but paid her fare and sat down. The bus driver was James Blake, a young man recently back from World War II. Blake refused to drive the bus. He told her that she would have to exit the bus and reenter at the appropriate door, as the rules said, in the back. After Rosa exited, Blake refused to open the rear doors, then drove off, and left her. He was trying to teach her a lesson. She had a long walk home.

Twelve years later, the same bus driver, though Rosa did not realize it at the time, was driving when she got on board after working at a department store. She paid her fare and sat in an empty seat in the first row of back seats reserved for blacks in the "colored" section. As the bus traveled along its regular route, all of the white-only seats in the bus filled up. When the white section filled up, bus drivers were supposed to reassign seats for the whites.

Blake noted the front of the bus was filled with white passengers and there were two or three white men standing. He then moved the "colored" section sign behind Rosa and demanded that she and three others give up their seats in the middle section so the white passengers could sit down.

According to Rosa Parks, *When that white driver stepped back toward us, when he waved his hand and ordered us up and out of our seats, I felt a determination cover my body like a quilt on a winter night. When he saw me still sitting, he asked if I was going to stand up, and I said, 'No, I'm not.' And he said, 'Well, if you don't stand up, I'm going to have to call the police and have you arrested.' I said, 'You may do that.'*

In her biography, *My Story,* she would later write,

> *People always say that I didn't give up my seat because I was tired, but that isn't true. I was not tired physically, or no more tired than I usually was at the end of a working day. I was not old, although some people have an image of me as being old then. I was forty-two. No, the only tired I was, was tired of giving in.*

She wasn't aware of it at the time, but her taking a stand by remaining seated gave permission for others to do likewise starting an entire movement.

In April of 1963, marches and sit-ins in Birmingham led to the arrest of many including Dr. Martin Luther King. In protest of the protests, seven pastors and one rabbi wrote an editorial encouraging this alternative course of action,

> *When rights are consistently denied, a cause should be pressed in the courts and in negotiations among local leaders, and not in the streets. We appeal to both our white and Negro citizenry to observe the principles of law and order and common sense.*

Dr. King responded from his jail cell in Birmingham, Alabama,

For years now I have heard the word, "Wait!" It rings in the ear of every Negro with a piercing familiarity. This "wait" has almost always meant "never." It has been a tranquilizing Thalidomide, relieving the emotional stress for a moment, only to give birth to an ill-formed infant of frustration. We must come to see with the distinguished jurist of yesterday that "justice too long delayed is justice denied." We have waited for more than 340 years for our constitutional and God-given rights. The nations of Asia and Africa are moving with jet like speed toward the goal of political independence, and we still creep at horse and buggy pace toward the gaining of a cup of coffee at a lunch counter.

Robert Fritz in *The Path of Least Resistance* describes two approaches to life that illustrate the fundamental difference between the religious leadership in Birmingham and Dr. King.

The religious leaders in Birmingham were working from what Fritz labels as *the reactive/responsive approach to life* where circumstances determine actions. The religious leaders were frustrated at the chaos and responded by protesting the marches and encouraging patience and faith in the current legal system to settle any injustices.

As an alternative to *the reactive/responsive approach to life,* Fritz offers *the creative/generative approach to life* where choices are made rooted in a vision the person is trying to create for him or herself, or for the world. People who live from this approach are not limited by their situation or even the actions of others, instead they are empowered by their visions and values. Dr. King was not driven by circumstances or the choices of others, but by something greater, a vision for what might be, a vision he expressed magnificently during The March on Washington in August of 1963. All he needed was a little encouragement to let his light shine. During his sermon at the March on Washington, a voice to the side, Mahalia Jackson, urged him, "Tell them about the dream, Martin." From there, he left the written text of his speech looking beyond what was to what might be, telling everyone what he saw,

> *I have a dream that one day this nation will rise up and live out the true meaning of its creed: "We hold these truths to be self-evident, that all men are created equal."*
>
> *I have a dream that one day on the red hills of Georgia, the sons of former slaves and the sons of former slave owners will be able to sit down together at the table of brotherhood...*
>
> *I have a dream that my four little children will one day live in a nation where they will not be judged by the color of their skin but by the content of their character.*
>
> *I have a dream today!*

Dr. King spoke not of a dream in some far off future, but a Kingdom of God present, real, and possible. He could see it, and he shared it.

Jesus was also a dreamer. When Jesus appears in the Gospel of Mark, the first thing he says is, "The Kingdom of God is near." Then he points out the kingdom everywhere. "The Kingdom of God is like that sower going out to sow his seed..." "The Kingdom of God is like a landowner hiring workers..." The Kingdom of God is like someone throwing a banquet...", like "a merchant seeking fine pearls," "like a mustard seed," over and over. Jesus saw the Kingdom of God all around him, exemplified in new ways every day. Jesus' expectation of his followers was not only that they would pray, "Thy kingdom come," but that they would see it and live it into reality.

The Anxious Crowd

Here is another test. Do you recognize this group?

These circles represent the magi from the account of the birth of Jesus in the Gospel of Matthew. They came into Jerusalem at the time of Roman occupation and the rule of King Herod. Pay close attention to the emotional response of Herod and Jerusalem to these strange visitors from afar. Here is the beginning of their story from Matthew 2,

> In the city of Jerusalem, in the era of Herod the King, when Jesus was a baby, wise men, studiers of the stars, came from the East into the capital.
> The magi walked into Herod's palace and asked, "Where is the baby who has been born, the new king of the Jews? We have been watching the skies and have seen his sign, the new star in the sky, and have traveled all this way to honor him."
> When King Herod heard the magi's question about the new king, he was frightened, and all Jerusalem with him.

How can a whole city respond in anxiety to what the king hears? Remember our images for a crowd, as overlapping circles where the boundary of one is not distinct from another. When there is no space between the emotional boundaries of people, the emotional energy runs like electricity through power lines from pole to pole, faster than sight. Like pool balls racked together on a table, strike one and they all move like a stadium of fans for the home football team. Once their team scores, the emotion travels through 80,000 or more, magnified along the way.

 My favorite image of a crowd's emotional energy is a herd of gazelle in Africa. Imagine a single animal sticks his head up, points his ears, and thinks "Lion?" and pretty soon the whole herd runs instinctually, whether there is a lion or not. If they could speak to their movements, as to why a particular animal ran when others ran, a single gazelle might say, "Well, with everybody running, it must be something terrible."

When Herod heard, "Messiah!" he thought like a gazelle, "Lion!" In all that follows, the city and Herod are driven by their collective emotion. That emotion motivates Herod, as it does all leaders who serve at the pleasure of the crowd, to protect what they have. When a leader is fused in as part of a crowd, and the anxiety runs through, no matter how rational and calm they act, as Herod does with the magi, whether a national leader or a parent in a family, the leader becomes a product of the anxiety of the whole.

It's easy to have emotion of others run through you in a family, in a nation, and even more so in a crowded boat during the middle of a storm while waves crash against the sides of the craft and flood the floor. See how the emotion spreads through the disciples in this boat excursion of Mark 4,

> *When evening came, Jesus told the disciples, "Let's go across to the other side." So, they left the crowd behind and started across the water. The other boats were with them.*

An unexpected windstorm arose, the waves smashed into the boat, water came over the side, the boat was filling. Jesus was asleep in the stern, on a cushion.

They yelled, 'Teacher, do you not care that we are perishing?"

Jesus awoke and rebuked the wind and the sea, "Peace!" He shouted, "Be still!" The wind ceased. The waters stilled. Then he said to the disciples, "Why are you so frightened? Do you still not have any faith?"

In this story, the storm is not only within each disciple, but moves like the wind between them, from each to each, gaining intensity as the whole group becomes afraid. For good or ill, emotions unify people into one uniform group. The disciples in the story of the storm act as one as they turn toward Jesus in fear and anger. Jesus is asleep symbolizing lack of worry. Like any anxious group, they can turn on even the most beloved and the most innocent, in this case the disciples turn on Jesus. They do not reach out in connection in hopes of some miracle, but instead they emotionally strike out in anger and fear. They become the storms in their minds. As a person who says, "I am angry," or "I am afraid," the 'to be' verbs show that he or she has become their anger or their fear. The disciples, unified in their emotion, wake Jesus up to accuse him, "Do you not care that we are about to die?!?" and essentially, "What is wrong with you?!?"

Somewhere, we've associated compassion as adopting the passion of another even if it is fear. Such care becomes, "If you are upset, I will be upset with you." "If you are appalled and angry, I will be angry with you." "If you are in an emotional storm, I will be stormy with you." "If you are terrified, I will be terrified with you." The result is that instead of being a present stillness, we have magnified the storms in others and empowered those dominated by their own emotions or the emotions of the group. When leaders offer empathy and share the emotion of the other person, they often affirm their belief in the storm and the emotions that accompany it. For many, storms are their addiction. Only in a storm do they feel significant and alive. For example,

The local mail carrier took a shortcut through a meadow on his bicycle. Midway across, a bull spied him and gave chase. The poor fellow barely made it to the fence.

A neighbor who watched him commented, "That bull nearly got you, didn't he?"

The postman replied, "Yes, nearly gets me every time."

The postman continually takes his route through the bull's field. Compared to the monotony of the same route every day, being chased by the bull creates an emotional storm that makes him feel alive. You can try and talk him out of it, but without some other experience to fill the void in his life, he'll likely not listen. Some people argue, fight, even abuse others for the same reason – it makes them feel alive.

In families, churches, and nations there will be emotional and even physical war over the tiniest and silliest things because of the energy the emotion gives them. They have no calling or vision besides. The alternative seems like death which is why such conflicts can be so volatile.

A friend and I went to help consult with a group of church leaders who were experiencing conflict over the selection of hymns for the later of two services. People were angry and not talking to each other. They wanted us to come in and listen to the complaints person by person. We asked, "When was the last time you evaluated your purpose, your mission?" They couldn't remember. We suggested they work on their vision and purpose because our experience had been that a church who knew why they existed would die for each other, but a church without a mission would emotionally kill each other, often for little or no reason. Emotions can spread through the whole community with leaders turning control of the church over to those who live for the 'running of the bulls'.

Church leaders can foster storms and the magnification of emotion within a congregation. When people come visit a church, some say, "We're church shopping. We weren't happy at our old church." The reply is often, "You weren't happy at your former church? Oh, well, you'll be happy here." What if they are never happy? What if being unhappy and upset about something is what makes them feel alive?

Leaders who are willing to be responsible for the happiness of others can take emotional storms and magnify them within the whole group. Edwin Friedman in *A Failure of Nerve* says the major factor undermining the growth and health of groups today is an over-developed sense of empathy, where people get upset when others are upset. He said that the worst counselors and leaders today are those who can't deal with the pain of others. Friedman calls this type of leader a "peacemonger," which he defines as,

> *...a highly anxious risk avoider, someone who is more concerned with good feelings than with progress, someone whose life revolves around the axis of consensus, a "middler," someone who is so incapable of taking well-defined stands that their "disability" seems to be genetic, someone who treats conflict or anxiety like mustard gas—one whiff, on goes the emotional gas mask and they flit. Such leaders are often "nice," if not charming.*

In order to keep the group together, these leaders turn over the organization to,

...the people who are crying the loudest, the chronic whiners, the organizational terrorists... the chronically angry, negative, and/or sullen... These also can be people who introduce terms like "trust," "empathy," and "consensus." Their agenda is to have others adapt to them. If leaders are not careful, a lot of hand wringing can go into, "I wonder what so and so will think?" If leaders are not vigilant, the dependent persons in organizations can wind up calling the shots.

When they awoke Jesus in the boat, the frightened disciples turned their emotion in frustration toward him and at him. Jesus had a couple of choices. He could have owned their emotion. Accepted that their fear was his responsibility and replied, "I'm sorry you're so afraid. How could I sleep during the storm?" He could have returned their emotional intensity with his own, and walked on water and left them.

In the boat, Jesus was able to be present with the disciples without adopting their emotion, being responsible for their fear, or returning the energy they directed toward him back at them. He was still. He was peaceful. Which allowed a miracle to happen. Stillness, in the midst of a storm.

The Crowd with a Cause

Guess what this is...

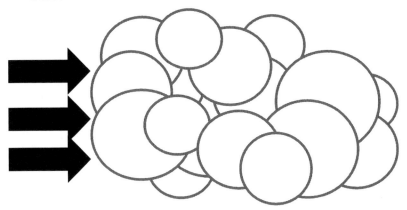

This is a crowd on the move.
The text is Mark 10,

Jesus, his disciples, and a large crowd left the town of Jericho. On the road on the outer edge of town was a blind beggar named Bartimaeus.

When Bartimaeus heard Jesus was coming, he shouted out to him, "Jesus, Son of David the King, have mercy on me!"

Many people told him, "Shut up. Jesus doesn't want to see you." That didn't stop Bartimaeus, he yelled louder, "Son of David the King, have mercy on me!"

Jesus stopped in the road and listened, then directed those around him saying, "Call him here."

The crowd spoke to the blind man, "Good news, get up. Jesus is calling you." Bartimaeus threw off his coat he had wrapped around him and jumped up and went to Jesus. Jesus asked him, "What do you want me to do for you?"

Bartimaeus replied, "My teacher, I want to see again."

"Go," Jesus said, "your faith has made you well." Immediately, he could see, and he followed Jesus on the way.

In this passage, a crowd comes out of Jericho with Jesus and his disciples. The crowd is on the move. They are marching. They are going somewhere, though it is not clear where. They have the emotion of a crowd at a concert or a football game. They are excited. Jericho is known in the Bible for its walls. In the Book of Joshua, the Israelites march around the city for several days and then God knocks the walls down. Likely, many new walls had been built around the city and within dividing the community by rigid separations. With Jesus, they unite in a godly cause and start moving picking up momentum.

Bartimaeus is blind. He is on the road outside of town. Perhaps he was ushered outside of town because Jesus was coming. In Atlanta, before the Olympics, many homeless were ushered from downtown because they hurt the image of the city. Likely Bartimaeus was moved outside the walls for the same reason. Bartimaeus hears that it is Jesus and calls out. "Jesus, son of David, (which means king) have mercy on me."

The crowd yells for him to, "Shut up!" Don't think too badly of them. This is what crowds do. For them, they are driven by a cause, a part of something important. They are out with Jesus, out to change the world, save their nation, their people, on a mission from God. For a crowd in motion there are simply two groups of people: those who are energizing our emotional movement and those who are blocking our way. Crowds love simplistic mechanical perspectives. Like cars on a highway, you're either moving with us or slowing us down. Move with us, and we will tolerate you, but slow us down and we'll offer you our contempt and the best curse we can muster. After all, they are marching. They are moving. Blind people can't go on journeys like that.

Then, Baritmaeus does something brilliant. He calls out to Jesus. He doesn't try to slow down or even speak to the crowd. It is of no use, and he knows it. He calls out to an individual, to a single person, "Jesus!"

As I mentioned before, crowds exhibit what is known as the *Genovese Syndrome*, or more simply, the *Bystander Effect*. The nature of crowds is simply this, if you are a victim, getting beaten or mugged, the more people in the crowd around you, the larger the number of bystanders, the less likely the crowd is to move and help.

There are countless examples of bystanders who watched while someone was beaten, abused, and even killed and later the individuals could not explain why they did not step out to help. It seems that, in a crowd, the brain looks to others for signals when trying to make sense of something horrible. The analysis by each brain is that what is in front of them can't be as terrible as it seems or else someone would move, since no one is moving it can't be that bad. Like the Tin Man in *The Wizard of Oz,* they retain their human shape but stand frozen. No one moves. The abuse continues right in front of them.

If you are ever in a situation when you need help from a crowd, do what Bartimaeus does, speak to one person. The movement of one person can awaken a whole crowd. Jesus acts. He notices Bartimaeus. He commands the crowd, "Call him here." The crowd fluctuates in attitude and behavior instantly. Bartimaeus goes from being a barrier to their cause to being their cause all because Jesus notices him, Jesus sees him, and with the attention of Jesus the celebrity, they feel differently about Bartimaeus. Before, they demanded him to, "Be quiet," and "Stay out of the way." Now, they speak kindly, "Good news. He's calling you."

The crowd's emotions change. They are willing to make Bartimaeus their cause. They may start a *Help Bartimaeus Foundation, The Bartimaeus School for the Blind, The Bartimaeus Home for Beggars,* or just outright adopt him. Bartimaeus could talk about how hard it is being poor, speak at the Jericho Rotary Club Luncheon, share about how terrible others have been to him, he could take the role of victim and write letters to the editor of the *Jericho Journal,* all of which the crowd would likely now support, at least for a while. That's what crowds do, especially once they have celebrity endorsement like Jesus.

In 1985, due to poverty, drought, and hunger in Africa, a group of celebrities bonded together to draw the public's attention to the suffering in Africa in a very emotional campaign called, *We Are the World*. The emotional factor was huge. There was a song, a record, and a nationally televised benefit concert. Millions of dollars were raised, awareness was raised, and the emotional rush was like a wave. I bought the album and sent money. I felt like I was the world, I was Africa. I watched as plane after plane of food was sent. We were helping! I felt like I was part of a grand movement, though I went nowhere. But then the emotion moved onto something else. The people were less hungry. The celebrities moved onto other projects. The crowd dispersed. As far as I know, today, there are still hungry people in Africa.

Crowds go from one cause to the next. As Roman historian Tacitus observed, "Mobs have neither judgment nor principle, ready to brawl at night for the reverse of what they desired in the morning." As in the case of Bartimaeus, a crowd can totally ignore the needs of a person or a group of people, then suddenly over focus on them. A crowd in motion sees facilitators and barriers, but not people. They are willing to make Bartimaeus their cause because Jesus points to him. But they still don't see him. Nor do they see Jesus. For the crowd, Jesus isn't a person either. He is a celebrity. So when they tell Bartimaeus, "Good news, he wants to see you." You can hear the infatuation in their voices; the "he" is an emotional *he,* much like crowds always speak of celebrities.

Jesus does not try and help the crowd see. He focuses on the one person in front of him. Jesus asks him, "What is it you want me to do for you?" Ironically, the one who is on the true mission from God in the story is the one who takes time to stop, to encounter, to see the person in front of him.

If he would have been riding the wave of the crowd, he wouldn't have noticed the individual Bartimaeus. Lost in the crowd, leaders don't see single persons as Kierkegaard noted,

> *There is no one who has more contempt for what it means to be human than those who try to be professional leaders of crowds. If an individual approaches one of those leaders, the leader doesn't care about him or her. He or she is much too small a thing to care about. Arrogantly, the leader sends them away. There must be at least a hundred. And if there are thousands, then the leader bends before the crowd, bowing and scraping - what untruth!*

Jesus is not that type of leader. When Jesus was on the move with the crowd, Bartimaeus called out to him, "Jesus, Son of David" which is a kingly title but also a celebrity title, the name of one apart from the crowd, one above all others, but here, in this truly personal moment, Bartimaeus speaks to Jesus in a much more intimate way. Bartimaeus calls Jesus, "My Rabbi..." or "My Teacher..."

The crowd, which had so much force before, in this encounter have essentially disappeared. Before they were a mountainous barrier to Bartimaeus, now they are little more than a mist around him. All that exists is Jesus and Bartimaeus. "What do you want me to do for you?"

Bartimaeus replies, "Teacher, I want to see." What Bartimaeus asks for is what Jesus is able to give. Bartimaeus sees again.

The story gives us a nice comparison at the end. Bartimaeus follows Jesus on 'the way'. This is different from the road or highway the crowd moved with Jesus as they came out of town. The followers of Jesus were known early on as people of 'the way.' They are people known for light, for vision, for connection, for sight, and for insight. While the crowd had its cause, one person got Jesus' greatest gift – vision. People with vision were what Jesus unleashed to transform the world.

The Massive Crowd

Can you guess what character this is and from what Bible story?

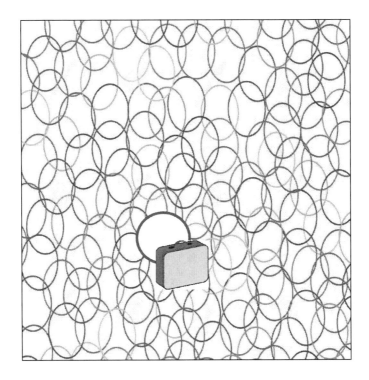

Here is a hint: inside that mob of circles is a little boy with his lunch. The story is the feeding of the 5,000 people with five loaves and two fish, which, according to the gospel of John, came from one boy's lunch. The story is told in all four gospels, and the details vary. This is my paraphrase.

The disciples returned after Jesus sent them out in pairs. They were tired, so Jesus told them, "Let's go away to a quiet place to rest for a while." They boarded their boat and went across the water to a vacant place by themselves. But as they moved, the crowd moved. They hurried on foot, gathering so many others along the way that the deserted place Jesus and the disciples were heading toward wasn't deserted by the time they arrived.

As they went ashore, Jesus saw the crowd and had compassion on them. They reminded him of sheep without a shepherd. Even though they were tired and hungry, Jesus started teaching them.

The disciples noticed the people, the sun late in the sky, and that Jesus didn't seem to have a plan other than caring for the crowd. They didn't want to go back in the boat and row any more. They wanted to rest. So, they mentioned to Jesus, "This is a deserted place. The hour is late. We've all travelled long and hard to get here. On behalf of the crowd (and us), send them away before it gets too dark to see so they can spread out and go into the surrounding villages and buy themselves something to eat."

Jesus answered them with this very simple instruction, "You give them something to eat."

The disciples choked at what Jesus had said. They looked at the crowd. They thought of what food they had brought and what little money they had and the tremendous cost of feeding such a large crowd.

They asked Jesus in shock, certain he hadn't considered what he had said. He was tired, sad, and hungry like they were. Maybe he just needed a little help to analyse the situation, the size of the need and the scarcity of the resources available.

"Uhmmm, Jesus? Are we to go to the surrounding area and buy dinner? It would take eight months pay just for enough bread for this crowd to eat."

"Well," Jesus said, "how much food do you have?"

The disciples searched among themselves and the surrounding crowd and replied, "We have five loaves and two fish." Apparently, this came from a little boy who had brought some food with him.

Jesus said, "Have the crowd sit down in groups on the green grass. They were seated in groups of hundreds and fifties. Jesus took the offered loaves and fishes, looked upward to heaven, blessed the bread and broke it, and gave it to the disciples to start passing out. Then Jesus divided the fish among them to distribute as well. They divided the food among the groups who shared it. Everyone ate until satisfied. Then Jesus' disciples gathered up the leftovers.

Jesus shows insight in how crowds work. Jesus instructs, "Have them sit in groups." Here is why this is so important. A missionary was serving in China when a great famine swept through the region. The missionary and others arranged for delivery of food, but it took several weeks to arrive. When they announced the food was coming and that they would pass it out the next evening, by morning there was a large group of hungry people, thousands massed in hope. When the distribution began, a riot broke out in the crowd. Several people wound up being injured and a few killed.

The missionary was broken-hearted. What he had intended to be part of the answer had turned into another problem. That night he was so distraught he could not sleep. As was his custom, he found himself going to the Bible for consolation. Late that night, he read where Jesus encountered the 5,000 hungry people, and one detail stood out that the missionary had never noticed before. Jesus had the crowd sit down. "Brilliant!" he thought. Jesus managed a hungry crowd by having them sit down. A seated crowd can't riot and their emotion doesn't spread as easily from person to person.

The next morning he announced they would try again to redistribute the food but this time they would have everyone sit down first. This time there were no problems. People were able to get food but didn't hurt one another to get there. The missionary wrote back home about his renewed appreciation for the common sense of Jesus, his understanding of people and of crowds. Jesus knew how to live in this world.

Jesus also knew how people think. The crowd is massive, the disciples can feel the hunger of the mob as well as their own hunger and fatigue. The problem is overwhelming, "Send them away," they instruct and almost beg Jesus. The problem is so large that they want distance. They know they don't have the resources to even begin to address it.

Jesus magnifies their pain and anxiety when he instructs, "You give them something to eat."

They give Jesus their analysis of resources relative to need, but he doesn't care. Then Jesus makes it personal. He doesn't debate the problem at all, instead he asks them,

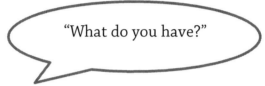

"What do you have?"

When a problem is so massive, and we know, in mechanical terms that we cannot fix it, we separate. We move to gated communities or form committees to talk about how terrible it is. If you read the stories together from the four gospels, then when Jesus asks, "What do you have?" the disciples don't mention their own food but respond with "There is a boy over here with five loaves and two fish." They use someone else's resources to address the problem.

The call of Jesus is not about what problems you can fix in the world, but this question,

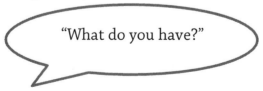

"What do you have?"

And once you answer this question, then you have to decide what you are going to do with it. You don't just buzz along with the crowd, you are called to see and do regardless of the outcome. Jesus doesn't give guarantees of effectiveness. Jesus wants lives of fidelity. If you are going to live THE YOU that God intends, you need to be able to do an accounting of what you have and put it to use. Your effort, may or may not solve any problems, it may or may not even come close, the ocean may remain so large and your boat still so small. Faith is not feeding 5,000 people with five loaves and two fish. Faith is TRYing to feed 5,000 people with five loaves and two fish, and hoping that God shows up in the process. It's not our job to do the impossible, miracles are up to God. Faith is saying, "Here is what I have. Let's see what we can do with it. Let's see what God can do with it." Encouraging others to not only do the same, but to join you as you encounter others along the way.

Because he is Christ, The Tiger, if you are brave enough to ask, "What do I have?" and pay attention looking near and far, what you are to do with it will be quite clear. It was to the little boy in John chapter 6. It will be to you.

A person in Nashville who has let her light shine and encouraged others to do the same is Tasha French Lemley. I met her at a men's study group. She came in and sat down in a chair, kicked off her shoes, crossed her legs beneath her, and told us her story. Here is what I remember.

Tasha moved to Nashville after graduating from college with her degree in graphic design. Since she had no experience in the field, no one would hire her. She took the only job she could find working at Kinkos, making copies, and crying daily that her life had fallen so far below her expectations.

On her way to work, she passed a homeless man regularly on a public bench by the sidewalk. She thought, 'If I passed the same person every day at a Starbucks, I would speak to them. I should speak to this man.'

She thought of what to say to him, so different from herself, and even rehearsed in front of a mirror questions she might ask.

They spoke regularly. From their conversations, she became curious about homelessness. She read Grand Central Winter by formerly homeless Lee Stringer who edited a New York street newspaper. She thought, 'What the homeless in Nashville need is a homeless newspaper. Somebody ought to start one.' Then she said, "I realized, 'Damn it! That somebody is me.'"

She started *The Contributor* with articles written by and sold by homeless or formerly homeless people on the streets of Nashville and surrounding communities. In 2012 The Contributor funnelled more than $2 million to homeless vendors in Nashville.

The beauty of Tasha's approach was that it started with one person crossing the distance and speaking to another. And today, throughout Nashville, *The Contributor* enables thousands of interactions daily between vendors and patrons. It also gives homeless people a voice in articles and art in the newspaper. The message is simple, everybody has salt, light, and something to share, everybody can contribute. She didn't try and solve the problem of homelessness, or even fix it in Nashville. Nor did she run away from the problem. She took what she had to share, and in doing so, created a city of contributors.

Christ, The Tiger keeps coming and keeps asking,

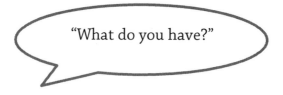

"What do you have?"

The Whole in One Crowd

Guess what this is.

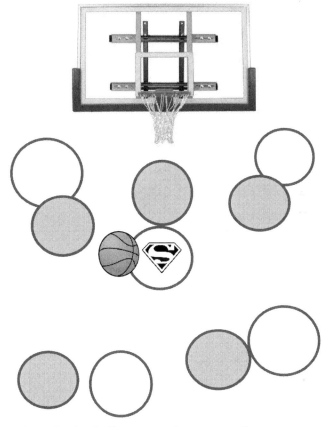

This is a basketball game when one player assumes the responsibility for the whole and tries to be the superstar.

John Wooden of UCLA was one of the most successful college basketball coaches. In a game, he would often have players run a full court press, this is when a basketball team doesn't fall back to defend their goal, but puts pressure on the ball handler and other players from the beginning of the play. The purpose of the press for many teams is to try and steal the ball. Not for Coach. If you happened to steal the ball, great, but that was not the real goal. Wooden's purpose was to have the other team hurry. Once a team got anxious and started to hurry, the best one or two

131

players would get frustrated and try and take over the game and forget their plan. In hurry mode, the best player would try and become a superstar or savior, the one would take the responsibility of the whole. No matter how good that player was, they couldn't beat Wooden's team alone, which is why Wooden's teams almost always won – always.

Wooden's philosophy for his teams was to be quick, but never hurry. When they didn't hurry, then they remembered the team concept. No one felt the pressure of the whole game. Each player understood his role in the whole and was challenged to live that in a flawless fashion. If they played in their space, their role, no one person could beat them. No matter how great the other team's 'star' was, no individual was better than five Wooden trained players working together. What Coach knew was, as soon as he could get someone playing savior, someone overfunctioning for the team, the rest would underfunction. The team plan and roles would be lost in the frenzy. When one person takes a large responsibility for the whole, or even another person in a relationship, it looks symbolically like this,

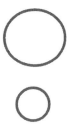

This is not of a mutual relationship but of an over/under relationship. One rises up and over-functions while the other under-functions, regardless of ability or role. Likely, the over-functioner believes that by stepping up, the other players will step up as well but an over functioning philosophy of leadership is seldom effective in a basketball game, a family, a church, congregation, or country.

Jesus challenges the "Do right, and you'll be rewarded" ideal. He also challenges the, "If you're just good enough, others will rally around you." In a team working together on roles, as one improves all improve and grow together. But no one can make others go when they don't want to grow. You cannot inspire the unmotivated and unless responsibility is the property of the whole, the one will bear it alone. If you try and change others by being 'good', the model is still one based on control. You are trying to shape others into your way by being good. The 'role model' of overfunctioning seldom works because when you are dependent on the underfunctioning changing, they are in control.

In the blended crowd mentality, individual roles and responsibility are unimaginable. Instead, they make one responsible for the whole. Watch the news tonight, how did a leader fail which will result in the destruction of all today? Watch a political campaign, especially for President, how many times does a candidate promise to save the economy, healthcare, the military, freedom, but never mention personal responsibility or ask voters to do anything other than believe – and vote!

This can happen in any system. A pastor can become responsible for the whole congregation, if he or she is charismatic enough, works hard enough, is 'good' enough, then the whole will rally. If a parent is good enough, then the children will come around. A parent often believes that by cleaning the house, the children will step up and help. Likely not. As a counsellor once advised, "Hell is the idea that there is such a thing as a 'good' parent."

Crowds make one responsible for the whole. They can adorn a king, queen, or hero responsible for fixing or saving whatever is wrong, and if there is a threat, a fear of loss, they will make one the scapegoat whose destruction is required for the rest to survive. The crowd is always willing to sacrifice the one for the many. Consider the plot to kill Jesus, **John 11,**

After the Pharisees heard that Jesus had raised Lazarus from the dead, the religious leaders called a meeting and anxiously asked, "What are we to do? Jesus is doing so many miraculous things! If we let him continue, everyone will believe in him and then the Romans will come and destroy The Temple and our nation!"

The High Priest, Caiaphas, said, "You know nothing! It is better for one man to die than to have the whole nation destroyed."

Sacrifice the one for the whole. As Caiaphas said, "It is better that one man die than to have the whole nation destroyed." In fear of losing all they held dear, they were willing to have Jesus killed, regardless of what good he was doing.

A healthy group, unlike the crowd, doesn't require one to be responsible for the whole, but instead each has a particular part to play. Again, remember the two soccer teams.

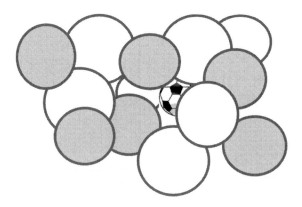

In the fused team, everyone is chasing the ball, there are no roles, and likely the team with one superior athlete will win every game.

In the mature team, the roles are clear, they are quick but don't hurry, and stick to their plan.

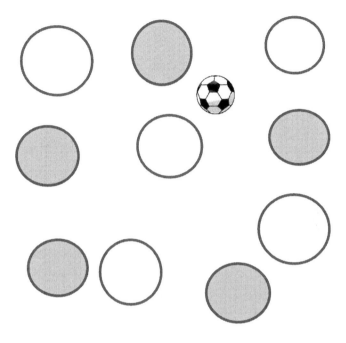

Here is a model from the early church that illustrates this concept in a similar way. See if you recognize it.

Paul wrote to the church in Corinth, 1 Corinthians 12,

The body does not have one member but important members. If the foot said, "Because I am not a hand, I do not belong to the body," that thinking wouldn't make it any less a part. If the ear said, "Because I'm not an eye, I do not belong," that way of thinking wouldn't make it any less a part of the body. If the whole body were an eye, where would the hearing be....

Now you are the body of Christ and individually members of it.

In a body mindset, like in Wooden's basketball team, the responsibility of the leader is not the entire family but the position of leadership. As long as the leader is trying to change followers, the followers are in charge. If the leaders functioning is dependent on the functioning of others, the others are in control. When a leader tries to change followers, they gain power. When a leader focuses on his or her role, and his or her calling and vocation, living into God's dreams for the world, then others will face their own power to choose and hopefully, claim their own potential and help others to do likewise.

Crowd Review

Who are the circles in this picture?

The smallest one is you, a long time ago. The larger ones are your parents or siblings or some strange circles from out on the street somewhere. Let me take you back in time. This is the story of your beginning on earth using insight from David Elkind, *A Sympathetic Understanding of the Child: Birth to Sixteen*.

When you were born, your parents said, "Oh, look, how tiny." As an infant, you could distinguish between loud sounds and soft sounds, between sweet and bitter tastes, between complex and simple visual patterns, and between objects that were moving and those that were still. What you could not distinguish was any difference between "you" and "not you." In your infantile mind, all was 'you'. 'Me' included everything your senses made known to you, your mother, father, any toys, and your hunger. You weren't the center of the universe, for in your infantile mind, you were the universe. Anything or anyone in your immediate experience existed and mattered and if it disappeared, it was gone. You did not cry when a toy left your sight, because for you, the object was only real when you saw it. Sensations from within or from outside of your body were the same. If a sharp object poked you, you did not understand that it was not part of you so you cried out without moving the arm or leg that was hurting.

Then your perception grew. You could remember objects even when you couldn't see or touch them. Even though out of sight, they still existed which at times could be disturbing and frightening, not only was part of your universe vanishing, out of reach, away and unattainable, but so was part of your self. When your mother left, the feeling was like an emotional amputation. The first few times you weren't sure you'd survive. Only when she went away and returned on many occasions could you learn to calm your own anxiety. The loss of a toy or a desirable object was similar. "Me" and "mine" became the same to you as you identified your sense of who you were with the people and the toys you knew. When one left your hands or your sight, it was as if you lost part of yourself.

As you age, and discover the difficulty of relationships, possessions can take the place of people. Crowds teach us to treat people like things; it's easy to start treating things like people. Who you are can get fused with objects as you become possessed by your possessions. Your crowd can become one like this one,

You can relate to your objects as if they are part of you, part of your crowd, as if they are people and relate to people as if they are objects. With today's technology, we can communicate to

others through our machines and not have to risk the vulnerability that goes with authentic relating, person to person. Bill Moyers described our present age this way, "Our children are being raised by appliances."

Family Systems Therapist Murray Bowen pioneered a scale to measure how differentiated a person is in their relationships between seeing everything as "me" or distinguishing between "me" and "not me". Looking at the Family as a fused system of individuals (a crowd), Bowen looked for a differentiated individual to help the family move toward health. I've taken the work of Bowen, Friedman, and others to summarize life lost inside the crowd and life out of the crowd as THE you, relating to God and others as persons, and life as potential.

In The Crowd

from Murray Bowen

High demands on relationships.

o   Often reactive to circumstances and people using much of life's energy reacting to circumstances and emotions of others. Little energy left to perceive potential choices and available possibilities.

o   High expectation of others. Perceive others as primary source for happiness.

o   Uncertain of personal value. Look to others for affirmation. Take on various personas based on groups.

o   Anxiously focus on perceptions of others. Wonder constantly what others are thinking or feeling.

o   Relationships are usually intense.

o   Protect group by preserving status quo with life and death intensity.

Instinctive reactions to problems, pain, and challenges.

o   React automatically and defensively rather than intentionally and thoughtfully.

o   Low tolerance for pain or uncertainly.

o   Low imagination to see other views or solutions.

o   Focus on failure of others discerning flaws and weaknesses.

o   Low sense of humor.

o   Tense, unable to relax.

o   Feel personally responsible for thoughts, feelings, and actions of others.

•   **High anxiety. Focus on comfort and calm instead of growth, learning, and development.**

•

Out of The Crowd

from Murray Bowen

Low demand on relationships.

o Seldom reactive.

o Reasonable expectations of others.

o Principle and goal oriented.

o "Inner" as opposed to "Outer" focused and directed.

o Confident in being able to love and being loveable.

o Not anxious about other people's opinions, thoughts, feelings, actions or reactions.

o Little regard to status hierarchies.

o Realistic assessments of self and others.

o Relationships are usually calm.

Thoughtful response to problems, pain, and challenges.

o Confident in own thoughts, beliefs, and values, but can consider other's views with respect and curiosity.

o Listens without reacting. Don't feel responsible for the emotions of others.

o Adaptive under stress.

o Able to assume responsibility for choices and actions without feeling responsible for emotions, choices, or reactions of others.

Low anxiety. Growth oriented. Comfortable with discomfort.

In The Crowd

from Robert Fritz

In *The Path of Least Resistance*, Robert Fritz points out two approaches to life: *The Reactive/Responsive Approach* and *The Creative/Generative Approach,* which offer us characteristics for life in and out of the crowd.

The Reactive/Response Approach is when circumstances are the driving force in your life. You either react against or respond to the situation. The circumstances, rather than your aspirations and values, are the driving force.

o   Quality of life is contingent upon external circumstances.
o   Power is outside, never within.
o   Generally cynical expecting the worst.
o   Have a short emotional fuse, often react suddenly.
o   Hold conspiracy theories about people in power.
o   Perceive life to be full of situations that require overcoming to survive.
o   Presume powerlessness in the world,

The Creative/Generative Approach focuses on the power individuals and groups to shape their lives and the world around them. In this approach, the driving force is not the situation you are in, but your desires, your aspirations, your vision, and your values.

o   Driving force in life is internal not external.
o   Choices shape a person's quality of life.
o   Visionary, not cynical.
o   Nonreactive. Don't have an emotional short fuse.
o   Don't hold conspiracy theories.
o   Has an enabled, creative imagination that envisions a world that might be. Asks, "What do I want to create?"

In The Crowd

from Henri Nouwen

Writer Henri Nouwen wrote about "the world" in a way very similar to the crowd as I am describing it. Using a collection of images pulled from Nouwen's writings, here are some helpful questions for reflection about life in the crowd.

o *Does a little criticism make you angry?*

o *Does a little rejection make you depressed?*

o *Does a little praise raise your spirits?*

o *Does a little success excite you?*

o *Do you feel there is a qualifier in your relationships and in your work, "I'll be appreciated if…" and that you face one 'if' after another each day?*

o *Is the attention, approval, and appreciation of others your addiction?*

o *Does it take very little to raise you up or thrust you down?*

o *Are you often like a small boat on the ocean, at the mercy of the crowd and its waves?*

o *Do you feel as if you are constantly going to others with the hidden emotional question, "Do you love me, accept me, appreciate me?"*

o *Do the voices of the crowds in your life control you and have all the power?*

o *Do you spend much of your time and energy trying not to get tipped over in your relationships, and your life feels like a struggle for survival, and anxious struggle rooted in the false idea that your crowds define you?*

Out of The Crowd

from Anne Frank

She was not a president or an inventor, she didn't save the world, her family, or herself, but was quite the tiger in a fearful and violent world.

I have one outstanding trait in my character, which must strike anyone who knows me for any length of time, and that is my knowledge of myself. I can watch myself and my actions, just like an outsider. The Anne of every day I can face entirely without prejudice, without making excuses for her, and watch what's good and what's bad about her... I understand more and more how true Daddy's words were when he said: 'All children must look after their own upbringing.' Parents can only give good advice or put them on the right paths, but the final forming of a person's character lies in their own hands.

I can't imagine how anyone can say: I'm weak, and then remain so. After all, if you know it, why not fight against it, why not try to train your character? The answer was: Because it's so much easier not to!

Sympathy, Love, Fortune... We all have these qualities but still tend to not use them!

No one has ever become poor by giving.

Where there's hope, there's life. It fills us with fresh courage and makes us strong again.

Out of The Crowd

from Rudyard Kipling

Rudyard Kipling's *The Law of The Pack* offers a sense of what it's like to be an individual in a family or team. This is a strong sense of "I" and a strong sense of "We" or "Us."

NOW this is the law of the jungle,
as old and as true as the sky,
And the wolf that shall keep it may prosper,
but the wolf that shall break it must die.

As the creeper that girdles the tree trunk,
the law runneth forward and back;
For the strength of the pack is the wolf,
and the strength of the wolf is the pack.

Kipling's *If* offers a wonderful illustration of life out of the crowd. I altered the final line. The original version follows.

IF

If you can keep your head when all about you
  Are losing theirs and blaming it on you,
If you can trust yourself when all men doubt you,
  But make allowance for their doubting too;
If you can wait and not be tired by waiting,
  Or being lied about, don't deal in lies,
Or being hated, don't give way to hating,
  And yet don't look too good, nor talk too wise:

If you can dream—and not make dreams your master;
  If you can think—and not make thoughts your aim;
If you can meet with Triumph and Disaster
  And treat those two impostors just the same;

145

If you can bear to hear the truth you've spoken
 Twisted by knaves to make a trap for fools,
Or watch the things you gave your life to, broken,
 And stoop and build 'em up with worn-out tools:

If you can make one heap of all your winnings
 And risk it on one turn of pitch-and-toss,
And lose, and start again at your beginnings
 And never breathe a word about your loss;
If you can force your heart and nerve and sinew
 To serve your turn long after they are gone,
And so hold on when there is nothing in you
 Except the will which says to them: 'Hold on!'

If you can talk with crowds and keep your virtue,
 Or walk with Kings—nor lose the common touch,
If neither foes nor loving friends can hurt you,
 If all men count with you, but none too much;
If you can fill the unforgiving minute
 With sixty seconds' worth of distance run,
Yours is the Earth and everything that's in it,
And, even more, you'll be Out of The Crowd, Beloved One!

Original ending: *And—which is more—you'll be a Man, my son!*

In The Crowd

from Ken Kesey's *One Flew Over the Cuckoos' Nest*

In Kesey's novel, the clinically insane seem to have a far clearer sense of life than the sanatorium staff. As only an artist of great skill can, his writing illustrates with great clarity life in and out of the crowd.

I'd think, That ain't me, that ain't my face. It wasn't even me when I was trying to be that face. I wasn't even really me then; I was just being the way I looked, the way people wanted. It don't seem like I ever have been me...

I remembered one thing: it wasn't me that started acting deaf; it was people that first started acting like I was too dumb to hear or see or say anything at all.

Like a cartoon world, where the figures are flat and outlined in black, jerking through some kind of goofy story that might be real funny if it weren't for the cartoon figures being real guys.

All that five thousand kids lived in those five thousand houses, owned by guys that got off the train. The houses looked so much alike that, time and time again, the kids went home by mistake to different houses and different families. Nobody ever noticed.

All I know is this: nobody's very big in the first place, and it looks to me like everybody spends their whole life tearing everybody else down.

Out of The Crowd

from Ken Kesey's *One Flew Over the Cuckoos' Nest*

He who marches out of step hears another drum.

I'd take a look at my own self in the mirror and wonder how it was possible that anybody could manage such an enormous thing as being what he was.

There's no doubt in my mind that McMurphy's won, but I'm not sure what.

The stars up close to the moon were pale; they got brighter and braver the farther they got out of the circle of light ruled by the giant moon

But he won't let the pain blot out the humor no more'n he'll let the humor blot out the pain

Then some guy wandering as lost as you would all of a sudden be right before your eyes, his face bigger and clearer than you ever saw a man's face before in your life. Your eyes were working so hard to see in that fog that when something did come in sight every detail was ten times as clear as usual, so clear both of you had to look away. When a man showed up you didn't want to look at his face and he didn't want to look at yours, because it's painful to see somebody so clear that it's like looking inside him, but then neither did you want to look away and lose him completely. You had a choice: you could either strain and look at things that appeared in front of you in the fog, painful as it might be, or you could relax and lose yourself.

Out of The Crowd

Various Quotes from Ralph Waldo Emerson

Do not go where the path may lead, go instead where there is no path and leave a trail.

Is it so bad, then, to be misunderstood? Pythagoras was misunderstood, and Socrates, and Jesus, and Luther, and Copernicus, and Galileo, and Newton, and every pure and wise spirit that ever took flesh. To be great is to be misunderstood.

Whatever you do, you need courage. Whatever course you decide upon, there is always someone to tell you that you are wrong. There are always difficulties arising that tempt you to believe your critics are right. To map out a course of action and follow it to an end requires some of the same courage that a soldier needs. Peace has its victories, but it takes brave men and women to win them.

The purpose of life is not to be happy. It is to be useful, to be honorable, to be compassionate, to have it make some difference that you have lived and lived well.

Life is a journey, not a destination.

Make the most of yourself....for that is all there is of you.

To laugh often and much; to win the respect of intelligent people and the affection of children; to earn the appreciation of honest critics and endure the betrayal of false friends; to appreciate beauty; to find the best in others; to leave the world a bit better; to know even one life has breathed easier because you have lived. This is to have succeeded.

About the Author

David Jones is a pastor and author of the following:

The Moment
there is no place like now

Enough!

The Psychology of Jesus:
Practical Help for Living in Relationship

Jesus Zens You
(Formerly published as
The Enlightenment of Jesus)

Moses and Mickey Mouse:david
How to Find Holy Ground in the
Magic Kingdom and Other
Unusual Places

For the Love of Sophia
Wisdom Stories from Around the World
And Across the Ages

Going Nuts! (Fiction)

For more information on these books,
go to: www.davidjonespub.com

The following are available for free on the website:
Prayer Primer and
In the Beginning Were the Words.

Contact David at: davidjonespub@outlook.com.

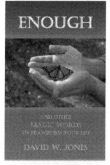

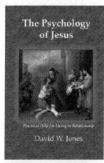

Made in the USA
Columbia, SC
15 March 2019